WANTED

by the FBI

THE FEDS AGAINST
A JEWISH LAWYER

ARTHUR MILLER

ISBN: 978-965-7041-29-1 (hardcover)
ISBN: 978-965-7041-30-7 (paperback)
ISBN: 978-965-7041-31-4 (e-book)

Publishing services provided by JewishSelfPublishing. The author acts as the publisher and is solely responsible for the content of this book, which does not necessarily reflect the opinions of JewishSelfPublishing.

www.jewishselfpublishing.com
info@jewishselfpublishing.com
(800) 613-9430

The author can be contacted at m9998279@bezeqint.net.

Printed in Israel

CONTENTS

DEDICATION

THE TRADITION OF AN AUTHOR dedicating his book dates back almost as far as the first printed books many centuries ago. I was told by many readers that my dedication for my first book, *Because It's Israel: An Aliyah Odyssey*, published in May 2019, brought them to tears. I do not intend this dedication to bring anyone to tears, but it is an honor that I do not take lightly.

When *Because It's Israel: An Aliyah Odyssey* was released, I had one very successful book launch in Beit Shemesh, Israel. Two days after the book launch, I met with a publicist to map out the advertising strategy and other publicity for my book. Soon after that meeting, before I could make any progress on my marketing plans, I tripped in my home, broke my hip, and had to be admitted to the hospital for surgery.

I spent the next week in Shaarei Tzedek Hospital in Jerusalem and five weeks at the Neve Amit rehabilitation facility in Rechovot, Israel. I became depressed there, as I was convinced that I would never walk again. I could not do anything that was asked of me — not even the simplest of tasks. I sat down and started to cry. My physical therapist, Atza, originally from Eritrea, came over to see why I was crying.

"I can't do anything with my leg. I will never be able to walk again."

Atza sat down next to me and assured me that she would have me walking again within a few weeks.

When I left the rehabilitation facility, I was walking, albeit with a limp and with the help of a walker.

I hugged Atza and thanked her from the bottom of my heart, not only for getting me back on my feet again but also for improving my self-confidence and, thus, helping me step out of my depression.

In gratitude, Atza is the first person to whom this book is dedicated.

Over a year has gone by since my fall, and although it is with a cane and a bad limp, I am walking. This very slow healing process, which my doctor assured me was normal, has limited my mobility in the many months that have passed since then. It has also prevented me from doing justice to marketing my first book, as I have been confined, for the most part, to my home.

In February, the coronavirus pandemic hit Israel, and as a person in the highest risk group, I was once again confined to my home for over two months while Israel was in total lockdown.

Despite experiencing some serious health issues that arose during the lockdown, I would not listen to my wife, Ronnie, when she suggested that I should go to the hospital for fear that I would be exposed to the coronavirus. Instead of seeking medical care at the hospital, I preferred the safety of my home.

Eventually, I could no longer postpone a visit to the hospital, and my doctor, Hillel Trope, who had been treating me over the phone, had nurse Nancy Hershkowitz come to my home to treat me and take blood tests. Dr. Trope then insisted that I be hospitalized. The actions of Dr. Trope and Ms. Hershkowitz helped me to recuperate and return home to finish this book.

Thus, I thank both Dr. Trope and Ms. Hershkowitz for taking care of me at that time by also dedicating this book to them.

I spent almost five days at Shaarei Tzedek Hospital being treated by faceless doctors and nurses (because they all wore masks), both Arab and Jewish, who put themselves at risk by working at the hospital during the pandemic.

Therefore, I am also dedicating this book to them and to all the workers in the healthcare system. They are all doing justice to the Hippocratic Oath.

Last but certainly not least, I dedicate this book to my life partner, my incredible wife Ronnie.

Not only has she cared for me these fifty-three years of our marriage, but over the past year, she has gone above and beyond the call of duty, as she has been there for me in everything while I have struggled to return to normal mobility and activity.

What is even more amazing is that this wonderful woman, who finds driving in Israel a daunting task, has not hesitated to visit me at the rehabilitation facility, visit me at the hospital, or take me wherever I need to go — driving by herself.

Well done!

Arthur Miller
Beit Shemesh, Israel
February 2021/Shevat 5781

To Jonathan,
Welcome home!

INTRODUCTION

THE STORY THAT FOLLOWS IS a true story. I know that because I lived and experienced all of the events related in these pages. The facts and incidents related in this book mostly occurred between 1968 and 1976. For nearly fifty years, I have told only a few people the details of this story.

Whenever I have shared these events with friends, they have told me that I should write a book, but I refused because I preferred to keep these events to myself.

However, over the years, particularly with the termination of the presidential terms of William Jefferson Clinton and George W. Bush, there seemed to be a plethora of presidential pardons and commutations for all sorts of criminals, regardless of the seriousness of their crimes.

For example, during his eight years in office, President Clinton pardoned 456 people, including Marc Rich, who had been convicted of wire fraud, mail fraud, racketeering, racketeering conspiracy, criminal forfeiture, income tax evasion, and trading with Iran in violation of the trade embargo.

President George W. Bush pardoned 200 people, including Lewis "Scooter" Libby, who was an assistant to the President and Chief of Staff to Vice President Dick Cheney. Libby had been convicted of perjury in connection with the scandal that outed CIA officer Valerie Plame.

All of these pardons, however, paled in comparison to President

Barack Obama, who pardoned or commuted the sentences of 1,927 people, including two individuals whose commutations caused me to rethink my decision regarding the telling of this story.

The first commutation was granted to Oscar López Rivera. Mr. Lopez Rivera was the suspected leader of the Fuerzas Armadas de Liberación Nacional Puertorriqueña (FALN), a militant group seeking to force the United States to grant independence to Puerto Rico, a territory belonging to the United States.

Between 1974 and 1983, FALN was responsible for more than 130 bomb attacks in the United States. In 1981, Mr. López Rivera was found guilty of multiple crimes, including seditious conspiracy, use of force to commit robbery, interstate transportation of firearms, and conspiracy to transport explosives with intent to destroy government property.

On January 24, 1975, a bomb exploded at the height of the lunch hour in historic Fraunces Tavern in lower Manhattan, the former headquarters of General George Washington during the American Revolution. FALN claimed responsibility for the bombing in which 4 men were killed and 43 more were injured.

Mr. Lopez Rivera was apprehended in 1981 and was sentenced to 55 years in federal prison. In 1988, he was sentenced to an additional 15 years for conspiring to escape from prison.

The second individual to have her sentence commuted during President Obama's last days in office was Chelsea Elizabeth Manning. Ms. Manning, a member of the United States Army, was court martialed and convicted in July 2013 of violations of the Espionage Act and other offenses, including disclosure to WikiLeaks of nearly 750,000 classified (or unclassified but sensitive) military and diplomatic documents. She was imprisoned from 2010 until 2017, when President Obama commuted her sentence to time served. Despite the commutation, Manning is currently in jail for her continued refusal to testify before a grand jury against WikiLeaks founder Julian Assange.

The charges against Manning included aiding the enemy, which was the most serious charge and could have resulted in a death sentence.

She was sentenced to 35 years at Fort Leavenworth, a maximum-security prison. On January 17, 2017, President Barack Obama commuted Manning's sentence, and, but for her refusal to testify before a grand jury, she would have been released after serving just 7 years of her 35-year sentence dating from her arrest on May 27, 2010.

In explaining his reason for commuting Manning's sentence, President Obama indicated that he felt that the 7 years she had served had been enough.

Both Manning and López Rivera received favorable presidential action with respect to their criminal activities. However, in my mind, those criminal activities categorized them as enemies of the United States. At the same time, another individual, Jonathan Pollard, a Jewish intelligence officer, languished in a federal prison for more than 30 years, as consecutive presidents could not bring themselves to release Mr. Pollard.

Apparently, President Obama thought the 7 years that Manning served had been enough, but the more than 30 years served by Jonathan Pollard were not enough to move Obama to act on Pollard's behalf. Mr. Pollard pleaded guilty to espionage, as he passed secrets to a friendly nation, Israel. The judge ignored the terms of the plea bargain between Pollard and the United States Department of Justice and sentenced him to life in prison, making Pollard the only person to receive a life sentence while spying for a friendly country.

Still, except for an occasional letter to the editor in the Jerusalem Post in support of Mr. Pollard, I kept my silence. Even after his release on parole in 2017, the United States government imposed significant restrictions on Pollard's movement, thereby limiting his employment opportunities. Of greater consequence was the fact that the United States government denied requests that Pollard and his wife, now in their 60s and in failing health, be allowed to make *Aliyah* as soon as their medical conditions improved enough for them to be permitted to travel.

The government's treatment of Jonathan Pollard reminded me of the events of 50 years ago, when the United States government refused to negotiate with me concerning the release of Rabbi Meir Kahane, who was serving a one-year sentence in a halfway house in New York, in exchange for information that might have aided in the capture of the FALN terrorists.

Instead, unbelievably, as a result of my representation of an individual who believed he had information about the Fraunces Tavern bombing, which I was willing to exchange for Rabbi Kahane's release from prison, I became the target of the United States government in the Fraunces Tavern bombing investigation. No matter how hard I tried to rationalize the events, I could only conclude that my treatment and that of Rabbi Kahane was the result of government-sanctioned anti-Semitism on the part of the United States. With the release of López Rivera, the mastermind behind the Fraunces Tavern bombing, the memory of my status as being "wanted by the FBI" came back to haunt me. I could no longer remain silent, so I decided to tell my story.

As I started to speak openly about my experience so many years ago, I was encouraged by my audiences to write this story. While speaking to groups in Israel, many people thought the story should be made into a movie, but when the audience got into a heated discussion about who should play me in the movie (most people thought Robert Redford was perfect for the role, while I only wanted my part to be played by Brad Pitt), I decided a book would be a better medium.

Except for several individuals whose names are a matter of public record, the names used herein may not be accurate. I simply do not recall many of the names of those individuals who played a part in my story after nearly 50 years have passed.

*Sample Reactions to Obama's Actions
on His Last Days in Office*

Chicago Tribune
January 19, 2017

The Obama pardon you should be mad about:
Oscar López Rivera

POLITIFACT
August 26, 2017

Former President Barack Obama "pardoned a traitor who gave U.S. enemies state secrets – he also pardoned a terrorist who killed Americans."

FOX NEWS FLASH
July 13, 2020

Where was the outrage when Obama commuted sentence of convicted terrorist?

- 1 -

FEBRUARY 1975

IT WAS A COLD AND dreary winter day in New York, and I had just arrived at my office at 280 Park Avenue in New York City. I was still enjoying a hot cup of coffee when my phone rang. It was our receptionist, who informed me that a United States marshal was in the office and had requested my presence.

While it was not that uncommon for a United States marshal to deliver subpoenas to members of the firm when our clients were under investigation, I was unaware of any reason why the marshal would want to see me.

Thus, my first reaction was that Denise, the receptionist, was joking with me. When I hesitated to say that I would be right out, Denise advised me that she was not kidding and that I should come to the lobby as soon as possible.

Out I went, and sure enough, there was a United States marshal in full uniform with a firearm at his side. He approached me and said, "Are you Arthur Miller?"

"Yes," I replied. "What can I do for you?"

He proceeded to hand me a subpoena, and, in front of a whole group of people in the lobby, he recited aloud that I had been ordered to appear before a federal grand jury the following morning at the Federal Courthouse at Foley Square in lower Manhattan.

"Are you sure you have the right party? What interest could the grand jury have with me?" I asked in surprise.

The marshal replied, "Your presence at the grand jury is required for you to give whatever information you have about the ongoing investigation of the bombing at Fraunces Tavern in which four people were killed."

Everyone in the lobby immediately looked at me in disbelief.

How could this nice, quiet, Jewish Orthodox tax specialist working in the tax department of a major international accounting firm have anything to do with a terrorist bombing in New York, responsibility for which had been claimed by FALN, a group that was seeking independence for Puerto Rico?

Not having much choice in the matter, I accepted the subpoena, and before I could even read it, news of the encounter spread through the office like wildfire.

On Thursday morning, as ordered by the subpoena, I arrived at the Federal Courthouse on Foley Square and proceeded to the grand jury room on the twelfth floor. Although I had been outside the grand jury room many times, this was the first time I was actually inside.

The grand jury is a large group of individuals (usually twenty-three) who meet when convened by a prosecutor, like the office of the United States Attorney, who presides over the grand jury meeting and presents evidence to the jurors concerning an individual or group of individuals so that the grand jurors can decide whether there is a basis for bringing criminal charges or an indictment against a potential defendant. Grand jury meetings are supposed to be confidential, and its proceedings are not permitted to be made public.

Lawyers representing clients who are appearing before a grand jury must wait outside the room. If their client needs to discuss anything with them, the client must leave the grand jury room to consult with them. The potential defendant who may be indicted as a result of the grand jury deliberations does not get to present any evidence concerning his innocence. Only the prosecutor is permitted to call witnesses, and the defense attorney cannot cross-examine them.

On this Thursday morning, I would be the one inside the grand jury room, and, as I had no indication of anything that would require me to have my own legal representation, I was there by myself. As I waited for the grand jury session to begin, I saw that the Assistant United States Attorney conducting the grand jury session was Henry Putzel III, with whom I had had many dealings over the years.

Following some opening questions of a general nature, Mr. Putzel started asking me questions that made me think that I should consult with my own counsel. Accordingly, I refused to answer several of Mr. Putzel's questions until I had an opportunity to seek the advice of counsel. Mr. Putzel then informed the grand jurors that he was taking me before a federal judge, who could order me to answer the questions under the threat of being held in contempt of court. As Henry and I walked from the grand jury room to the courtroom, where a trial was in session, my heart beat faster than I ever thought possible.

Fortunately, the judge felt that I had a potentially valid reason for refusing to answer Mr. Putzel's questions. The judge adjourned the grand jury session, ordered me to obtain my own counsel, and instructed me to reappear before him on Monday with my attorney prepared to argue the issues I had raised. On Friday morning, I had an appointment with Jacob Evsaroff, one of New York's leading criminal attorneys, who had agreed to represent me in this matter.

Hoping to get some work done before my appointment with Mr. Evsaroff, I arrived earlier than usual at my office. At 9:00 a.m., my phone rang. To my surprise, the call was from New York City bomb squad detective Santo (Sam) Parola who wanted me to know that he had heard rumors that I would be arrested due to my alleged involvement in the Fraunces Tavern bombing.

Regardless of what the United States Attorney's office thought I knew about the case, I did not have to reappear in court until Monday morning. Thus, I thanked the detective for calling me but assured him he was mistaken. Fifteen minutes later, he called me back to say that the New York office of the FBI had scheduled a news conference for noon, wherein they planned to announce a major arrest in the Fraunces Tavern case. Detective Parola had verified that I was the individual who was going to be arrested. To make matters even more difficult, Detective Parola indicated that, in coordination with the news conference, agents of the FBI would be at my office at noon and would be accompanied by news reporters and television cameras to film my arrest.

"How could this be happening to me?" I thought. "Someone in law enforcement was clearly in error."

How I got into this situation is my story.

- 2 -

GROWING UP

I N ORDER TO UNDERSTAND HOW I became one of the FBI's most wanted, it's important to understand my story — almost from the beginning.

My story begins on New York's Lower East Side. The Lower East Side, the southern portion of Manhattan Island, has a long history of being home to new immigrants to the United States. Beginning with German immigrants in the nineteenth century, who were followed by immigrants from Ireland, at the beginning of the twentieth century, the Lower East Side became a home to Jews looking for streets paved with gold or just fleeing persecution in Eastern Europe.

Perhaps it was the Lower East Side's proximity to Ellis Island that attracted more than 12 million immigrants entering America from 1892 until its closure in 1954. Perhaps it was the proximity of the neighborhood to the Statue of Liberty that made these teeming masses of immigrants feel welcome in America. Perhaps it was the housing provided by the hundreds of substandard tenement buildings that made it a convenient place for new immigrants to live.

I am sure all of these factors played a part in the development of the Lower East Side. By the time I was born in May 1944, the Lower East Side already had a rich history of providing shelter to the downtrodden Jews who had made their way there. In fact, when I was growing up on the Lower East Side, Jews had already started moving to the suburbs, with their place in the tenements being taken over by the ever-increasing Puerto Rican population.

The character of the neighborhood changed dramatically with the construction of what became known as the "co-ops," a massive development providing nearly 1,800 housing units in a series of buildings between 12 and 20 stories high. By 1949, when I was five years old, we were living in the labor union-sponsored Hillman Housing Corporation co-op apartments, which was a far cry from the decrepit tenement building in which we had lived on Sherriff Street.

Although our official address was 500A Grand Street, the three 12-story buildings comprising the 500 Grand Street complex were really on Willet Street, across the street from the landmark Bialystoker Synagogue, where I celebrated my bar mitzvah in 1957.

The Bialystoker Synagogue was a magnificent structure, built in the 1820s and repurposed from a Methodist church to a synagogue in 1905. The Bialystoker Synagogue was decorated with magnificent murals on the ceiling and beautiful walls in the women's section. In the corner of the women's gallery, there is a small break in the wall that leads to a ladder going up to an attic that is lit by two windows. Legend has it that the building was a stop on the Underground Railroad and that runaway slaves found sanctuary in this attic.

It was only after I moved to Israel in 2004 that I learned of a memorial plaque in the synagogue for Benjamin "Bugsy" Segal, one of America's most notorious gangsters in the early twentieth century. The plaque is situated next to a plaque in memory of Morris Lansky. Presumably, both of these plaques were put up by Meyer Lansky, another notorious gangster of the early twentieth century.

The neighborhood, running from FDR Drive (abutting the East River) to Essex Street, was a lower-to-middle-income area and was predominately inhabited by Jews. To the south and north were "the projects," populated by low-income households — predominately black and Puerto Rican families. To the west, on the other side of Essex

Street was New York's bustling Chinatown and Little Italy.

My brother Morris, or "Moish" as we called him, was three years my senior. He was enrolled in the local public school, and I have no recollection as to what constituted his "Hebrew" education through the third grade. When the time came for me to start my education, my parents took me to the Rabbi Jacob Joseph Yeshiva, a school for Jewish and secular studies about a half mile from our Grand Street apartment. "RJJ," as the school was known, was one of the first Jewish day schools in America. Founded in 1903, it served the Lower East Side as well as the greater Jewish community until it moved to Staten Island in 1969. Providing education from the first grade through high school, with a postgraduate program for rabbinical students, the student population exceeded a thousand students.

Before I could be accepted to RJJ, the principal of the school, Rabbi Dr. Hillel Weiss, had to interview my parents and me. Even 70 years after the interview, I recall him as a sweet and gentle person who I often referred to as a *tzaddik* — a saintly person. Rabbi Weiss told my parents that he would accept me in the yeshiva, and my parents agreed to the tuition of $5 per month. Rabbi Weiss then inquired as to the education of my older brother, Moish. Although I was only five years old at the time, I vividly recall my mother explaining to Rabbi Weiss that as much as they wished they could send Moish to RJJ, they did not think they could afford more than the monthly $5 tuition fees. Rabbi Weiss, anxious to provide my brother with a Jewish education, informed my mother that he had already agreed to the tuition of $5, but he had not decided how many children could attend RJJ for that amount. Thus, the following autumn, I started the first grade and my brother started the fourth grade at RJJ.

Yeshiva students endured long school days, as we carried "a double load." We had four hours of Jewish education, beginning at 9:00 a.m., with a fifteen-minute recess at 11:15 a.m. and a one-hour lunch break. At 2:00 p.m., we began our secular studies, which lasted until

6:00 p.m. These long days included Sundays. On Fridays, we were dismissed at either noon or, during daylight savings time, 1:00 p.m.

Located on Henry Street on the Lower East Side, RJJ was situated between two of New York's most prestigious high schools, Brooklyn Technical High School and Stuyvesant High School. Some of the best teachers in the New York City school system, who taught in these prestigious schools, found RJJ, which was just fifteen minutes away from each school, to be a wonderful place to supplement their income. Thus, this yeshiva that was always in financial difficulty managed to provide its students with access to some incredible teachers.

The long and distinguished list of RJJ alumni includes rabbis, doctors, lawyers, businessmen, and politicians. Rabbinical graduates include Rabbi Marvin Heir, head of the Simon Wiesenthal Center. Rabbi Heir has also won several Oscars for his movies produced for the Center.

Two rabbis from my class, Rabbi Avraham Kahn and Rabbi Herschel Reichman, are deans at Yeshiva University. Rabbi Avi Weiss (of my class) is a leading voice on a variety of issues of concern to the Jewish community. In 2013, Rabbi Weiss was recognized by Newsweek magazine as the tenth most prominent rabbi in America. Rabbi Weiss was Jonathan Pollard's personal rabbi and was active in raising awareness among the American public regarding the injustice of Pollard's sentence. Rabbi Meir Zlotowitz, another classmate, was the founder of ArtScroll Publications, a publishing house that has helped spread the words of the Torah among the masses. Another classmate, Sheldon Silver, was the speaker in the New York State Assembly for more than 25 years. The list goes on and on — all from the school on Henry Street on the Lower East Side.

Many alumni excelled in basketball at Yeshiva University, including Sheldon Rokach, who still holds the Yeshiva University record of 48 points in a single game. Another athletically inclined graduate, Simmy Reguer, played professional basketball in Israel for seven years, coached professional teams in Israel for over a decade, and now serves as a commentator on Israeli television broadcasts of United States NBA games. Our alumni list even includes Prof. Robert Aumann, a Nobel Prize winner, which is a distinction that very few schools in the world can claim.

In 1957, I entered RJJ High School. In my freshman year, I was the captain of the junior varsity basketball team, and the next year I made the varsity basketball team. In my senior year, I was captain of the varsity team. For those of us who were fortunate enough to play varsity basketball, the end of the regular school day brought with it two nights a week of basketball practice, when we arrived home at 9:30 p.m. to eat dinner and do our homework. After finishing the homework, if we had any energy left, we studied for any upcoming exams.

My mother reluctantly consented to permit me to join the varsity team on the condition that it did not affect my grades. If truth be told, my grades *were* affected, but my mother, knowing how important the basketball team was to me, did give me a little leeway in permitting me to remain on the team.

RJJ was a member of the Metropolitan Jewish High School Basketball League (MJHSL), and we played a full schedule of games, usually on Saturday nights. If we made the playoffs and advanced to the championship game, the ultimate prize — a game at Madison Square Garden as the opener to a New York Knicks game (provided the Knicks made the playoffs) — was awaiting us.

I remember those Sunday afternoons well, when the Knicks were playing their last game of the season and needed a win to qualify for the NBA playoffs, entitling them to another home game and, thus, a date to be filled by the MJHSL championship game. There we were, supposedly in our secular studies, huddled around those small transistor radios rooting for just one more Knicks victory so that we would get to play in the "Garden."

Throughout my three years of varsity basketball, I did get to play in Madison Square Garden once, and even now, 60 years later, playing at the Garden remains a lifetime memory.

Friday afternoon was our only time off, as we did not have secular studies on Fridays. After dismissal, we raced home, grabbed a bite to eat, changed into our sneakers and raced to the park on Broome Street, where, together with all the other RJJ students who were free, we played the "city game" of basketball. You needed to play at your very best, because if you lost a game, you either had to be picked by the person who had next (assuming you were one of the better players), or your day at the courts was over.

On many Fridays, our day at the park was interrupted by the latest group of immigrants to call the Lower East Side home, the Puerto Rican boys, who couldn't wait to fight us (literally) for the basketball courts. My brother and I ignored our parents' advice to leave the park before trouble started. Instead, we fought back to protect our turf. The police were often in our house trying to mediate the conflicts, but we believed that we could not let anyone push us around.

We had additional problems on our way home from school, when we had to pass through a small street known as Scammel Street. There was just one building on this street, and we were quite often attacked by kids who lived in the building there. Again, a policeman came to our home when my parents made a formal complaint. He advised us that the local priest was encouraging the youth there to attack Jewish kids. Shortly thereafter, the building was razed, Scammel Street disappeared, and our problems were solved.

Like most Jews of that period, we grew up in a household that was decidedly Democratic, where President Franklin D. Roosevelt was regarded as a savior of the Jews. As we got older, we learned of FDR's failure to do much for the Jews of Europe during the Holocaust as he steadfastly refused to open the gates of America to let the doomed refugees into the United States or to bomb the rail lines to Auschwitz to slow the Nazi death machine, which delivered 12,000 Jews to the gas chambers every day. This failure of the man our parents worshipped played a major role in the development of my political views.

I grew up believing in the cause of civil rights and often viewed myself as a future member of the NAACP, bringing justice to America's beleaguered black population. Growing up in New York and watching the evening news, as Southern governors attacked little black girls who wanted nothing more than go to integrated schools, how could a person be anything other than a potential freedom fighter, fighting for equality for our black citizens? Moreover, as an avid Brooklyn Dodgers baseball fan, didn't I owe a debt of gratitude to Jackie Robinson, Roy Campanella, Don Newcome, and the other black players who helped turn the "Bums" (as the Dodgers had been known) into winners?

Politically, I guess I came full circle in 1964 with the passing of the Civil Rights Act. I was working as a counselor in an orthodox Jewish Camp in White Lake, New York when the announcement was made that the historic piece of legislation had passed Congress. Under the Civil Rights Act of 1964, segregation on the grounds of race, religion, or national origin was banned in all places of public accommodation, including courthouses, parks, restaurants, theaters, sports arenas, and hotels. No longer could black people and other minorities be denied service simply based on the color of their skin. In all of the discussions concerning the Civil Rights Act, there seemed little doubt that the law had been designed to rectify years of injustice toward the black community.

Despite the clear provisions of the new law, which also barred religious discrimination, it seemed that Jews were not really part of the discussion as potential beneficiaries of the Act. As we all celebrated the news of this truly wonderful event in American history, one individual (me) rose and asked the assembled counselors and campers if anyone had analyzed if the passing of the new law was good or bad for Jews. Would these new rules come at the expense of

Jews who had only recently penetrated the walls of the large banks, insurance companies, Wall Street law firms, and the "big eight" accounting firms? These concerns were consistent with my upbringing, during which my mother addressed every issue or event by asking "Is it good for the Jews?"

I remember a story of a young boy who came home from yeshiva and excitedly informed his grandfather, who had just arrived in America, that Babe Ruth had hit three home runs that day. The grandfather responded to his excited grandson, "Tell me, Moishe, is what this Babe Ruth did good for the Jews?" All issues and news had to be analyzed with the same question: "Is it good or bad for the Jews?"

Whenever we heard on the news of some disaster in which innocent lives had been lost, my mother always wanted to know the names of the victims. I remember scouring passenger lists following an air crash or other tragedy to find out how many had Jewish-sounding names. While my mother was certainly sorry to hear of the loss of any innocent lives, if there were no Jewish names among the list of victims, my mother always said "thank God" that none of our co-religionists had been lost.

While still a student at the City College of New York, I rejected my Democratic upbringing and volunteered to work in the campaign of Republican mayoral candidate John V. Lindsay, only to become disillusioned when I discovered that the new Republican Mayor of New York was really a Democrat in disguise. In addition, my years at City College saw my first foray into the battle to free Soviet Jewry. By 1964, I had become aware of the plight of Soviet Jews, and, when a student organization invited a Russian diplomat to address the issue, several of the Jewish students at City College, including myself, prepared to debate the issue with this diplomat after his presentation. Although we all knew that the diplomat was lying to his audience, portraying Russia as the bastion of religious freedom, we were not successful in challenging his claims. He was so professional and charming that I knew we would not score any points for Soviet Jews that day.

Shortly thereafter, in a speech class, each student had to give a "speech to convince." Just about everybody gave their talk on working to expand the civil rights of our minority population. When it was my turn, I gave an impassioned speech in which I accused our parents' generation of sitting idly by while six million Jews were killed by the Nazis. I then said that another genocide was taking place in the Soviet Union, and I urged my class, Jews and non-Jews alike, to join in the struggle of the newly formed Student Struggle for Soviet Jewry (SSSJ).

In 1967, as a natural outgrowth of the civil rights movement, Mayor Lindsay decided to experiment with community control of local school districts. Under community control, instead of the education professionals controlling hiring, firing, curriculum, etc., this power was turned over to the locally elected school board. In the predominately minority populated communities comprising the Ocean Hill Brownsville neighborhoods in Brooklyn, the local school boards proceeded to transfer or terminate the largely white and largely Jewish teachers and replace them with minority teachers. What followed was a long and bitter strike that closed the New York City school system for months.

The issues pitted the white Jewish teachers and their powerful union, whose leadership consisted primarily of white Jews, against the black community school boards. Most experts believe that the resulting conflict was the cause of the rift in relations between Jews and black people in the United States that remains prevalent even today. Several Jewish teachers who were dismissed by the local school board refused to accept their situation and attempted to return to their jobs in the Ocean Hill Brownsville district, but Robert "Sonny" Carson, a militant black community leader, and his followers patrolled the school district, threatening the Jewish teachers with physical violence if they returned to their former schools.

One day, as I watched the news, a young rabbi known as Rabbi Meir Kahane, appeared and responded to these threats by announcing that his organization, the Jewish Defense League (JDL), which I'd never heard of before, would protect the teachers if anyone tried to harm them. As if by magic, the threats against the Jewish teachers stopped, and while the strike continued, there were no longer any pronouncements about beating up Jewish teachers.

Nevertheless, many Jews, mostly the elderly, poor, and those living in transition neighborhoods (predominately Jewish and mixed neighborhoods) found themselves victims of violent crime. Once again, Rabbi Kahane was on the nightly news, announcing that members of the JDL would provide security for those Jews who lacked the means to move from these rapidly deteriorating neighborhoods. These events caused me to investigate the JDL further, resulting in my joining by paying membership fees.

Paying those dues was the extent of my involvement with JDL, and as I embarked on my professional career, the JDL and its charismatic leader, Rabbi Meir Kahane, practically disappeared from my radar. Nevertheless, I could not ignore Rabbi Kahane's activities protecting Jews against rising anti-Semitism, as he or the JDL were constantly in the news. It seemed to me that the more that mainstream rabbis protested against Rabbi Kahane, the more publicity his actions received. While I strongly believed in the potential benefits of his actions for combatting anti-Semitism, I was just too busy to get involved with the JDL. I worked long hours, even taking night courses, with the end goal of being awarded a Master's in Law. I just did not have the time to be involved.

Nothing confused me more, however, than the affiliation of Rabbi Kahane with the newly formed Italian-American Civil Rights League (IACRL). In 1969, Mario Puzo wrote *The Godfather*, which soon became an international bestseller, bringing the terms "mafia" and "Cosa Nostra" and the idea of the Italian crime boss to the general public.

Soon, it seemed like every comedian had incorporated mafia jokes into his repertoire, and Italian gangster movies became commonplace, giving the impression that everyone of Italian descent was a gangster.

In April 1970, in response to these supposedly anti-Italian activities, Joseph Colombo, Sr., head of the Colombo crime family, publicly denounced what appeared to be open defamation against Italian Americans, resulting in the formation of the IACRL. The IACRL grew in popularity, and at the end of June, over 100,000 people attended a rally at Columbus Circle in New York. Prominent Italian Americans, including Congressman Mario Biaggi, addressed the rally. Shortly thereafter, in response to these activities, John N. Mitchell (President Nixon's Attorney General) and New York State Governor Nelson Rockefeller banned the use of the word "mafia" in official communications. Additionally, Ford Motor Company, a major sponsor of the hit television program *The FBI*, announced that the offending words would no longer be heard on the program. Producers of the forthcoming film *The Godfather* agreed to drop them from the script.

In 1971, as the IACRL increased its membership numbers and financial stability, Colombo announced that he was joining forces with Rabbi Kahane, claiming that both groups, the IACRL and the JDL, were being harassed by the federal government. This meeting of minds proved extremely beneficial to the JDL, as Colombo posted bail for arrested JDL members in amounts that the JDL could never hope to raise. Colombo then assigned his personal lawyer, Barry Slotnick, a leading criminal attorney (Barry referred to himself as "New York's greatest lawyer"), to represent Rabbi Kahane in his ever-growing legal issues with the United States government. For example, following his arrest on various criminal charges, Rabbi Kahane disclosed that Colombo once posted $45,000 in bail for him.

Explaining the JDL's association with Colombo and his group, Rabbi Kahane said, "Our only yardstick is what is good for the Jews, and this alliance is good for the Jews." Richard Rosenthal, former

NYPD undercover officer, told the press that Colombo also posted a substantial bail for eleven JDL members held on felony charges. Little did I know how useful and important this alliance would prove to be in the future.

On June 28, 1971, IACRL had its second rally in Columbus Circle. Before an estimated crowd of 150,000 participants, a black assailant stepped forth and shot Colombo in the head, seriously wounding him. He died seven years later, never fully recovering from his wounds. The assailant was killed on the scene, and no motive for the shooting, nor who ordered it, was ever discovered.

- 3 -

CAREER DECISIONS

FOLLOWING GRADUATION FROM RJJ, I spent the next four years getting a degree in accounting at the City College of New York (CCNY). I was not enamored with accounting, and America's involvement in the Vietnam war continued to increase, so I decided that my best career move would be to attend law school, specifically to pursue a career in tax law. In September 1965, I started my law classes at Brooklyn Law School with the goal of utilizing my undergraduate business education as much as possible.

I married Ronnie Hershcopf in September 1967, at the beginning of my third year in law school. Ronnie is from Brooklyn, and she was starting her senior year at Hunter College at the time, where she was majoring in French. We moved to the cooperative apartments on the Lower East Side, just a few short blocks from where I grew up. Ronnie supported us as a part-time teacher at Temple Emanuel in New York.

My grades in law school were much better than my grades in college, and I narrowly missed being selected for Law Review. In my last year of law school, as I faced the challenge of finding the right position to utilize my undergraduate business degree, I was excited when the FBI came to interview on campus. They were specifically seeking lawyers in the top 10% of their class with an undergraduate degree in accounting. I had been enamored with the FBI ever since I had gone to Washington in January 1964 with several friends during intersession and we'd taken a tour of the FBI headquarters. Accordingly, when the notice announcing the FBI's on-campus recruitment efforts was posted in my classroom, I took an application form and was overwhelmed by the volume of information they requested.

Unable to provide all of the historical family information called for in the application, I asked my mother if she could provide me with a family history that would help me get through the application. Much to my surprise, my mother took one look at the application and told me that she would not assist me in completing it. She had two reasons for her refusal. The first reason, which really shook me up, was that one of her good childhood friends had been Ethel Greengrass. At first, I did not understand the connection between Ethel Greengrass and my FBI application, but when she told me that Ethel's married name was Rosenberg, I understood her reluctance to help me with my application. Ethel Rosenberg, along with her husband Julius, were convicted of spying for the Soviet Union, and in 1953, they were executed in the electric chair in Sing Sing Prison for their crimes.

As the nation was still shaken up by the hearings held by Senator Joseph McCarthy of Wisconsin, my mother was deeply concerned that if this relationship came to light during any FBI investigation of the Miller family, I could jeopardize future employment opportunities not only for myself but also for my entire family. In addition, there were apparently some distant family members who may have been members of the communist party, whose identities my mother was not keen to disclose on an application form for the FBI. Without her help, I as unable to complete the application form. Thus, my hope of any career with the FBI was dashed. Little did I know the strange twist of fate that would get me closer to the FBI than I ever thought imaginable.

- 4 -

DISCLOSURE

WITH THE POSSIBILITY OF APPLYING to the FBI eliminated, I then considered applying to the "Big Eight" accounting firms that were carrying out on-campus interviews with people who had accounting backgrounds and who wanted a career in taxation. Representatives from all of the Big Eight firms came to my campus, and word quickly spread that if you wanted a career in taxation, these interviews were the best option.

After being interviewed by several of the Big Eight firms, I accepted a position with the second-largest accounting firm in the world, Arthur Andersen. Entry into the world of the Big Eight firms was a unique experience for a *shomer Shabbat* (Jewish Sabbath-observing) individual. To the best of my knowledge, I was either the first or the second *shomer Shabbat* employee of any of the Big Eight firms.

The issue of whether to disclose the fact that I would be leaving early on Fridays during the winter and that I would not be coming into work on Saturdays in a profession that was generally known to require a six-day working week was of major concern to me. And, of course, I was concerned about taking time off for the Jewish holiday of Passover, which often occurred at the same time as the deadline for filing taxes, which was often the busiest time of the year.

My first exposure to this issue arose quite by accident when I was in my junior year at CCNY. I accepted a part-time after-school position with a small Jewish accounting firm in midtown Manhattan, working approximately 15 hours per week. As I started the position in November, I never considered the need to work on Saturdays during the tax season (roughly February 1st to April 15th). Similarly, since I did not work on Fridays, the issue of finishing work early on Fridays also did not concern me.

As the tax season began, I was instructed that I should start coming into work on Saturday mornings, effective in February. After I told them that I was an observer of the Jewish Sabbath and could not come in on Saturdays, I was told that they would have to replace me but that I could continue to work until they found a replacement. By mid-March, I was still working. When I sought to clarify my status, I was told that I was doing such a wonderful job that they had decided I could continue to work for them. They rehired a previous employee to work on Saturdays.

For me, the lesson was clear: Do an exemplary job, and when you are faced with the issue of observing Shabbat and all the Jewish holidays, a solution will be found that will allow you to continue working at that firm. Thus, when I interviewed with the Big Eight firms and started working at Arthur Andersen in August 1968, I did not disclose my religious observances. Several people I knew who also interviewed with these firms and disclosed up front that they were Shabbat observers did not receive offers of employment. Because of these issues, a large percentage of *shomer Shabbat* accountants and lawyers worked for predominately Jewish firms, many of which (although they were certainly in the minority) tolerated these working habits.

My first conflict came during my second week with the firm while I was attending a three-week training course in Chicago. Classes were scheduled for Shabbat, and my instructor wanted to know why I was just sitting in the classroom and not doing any of the assignments. I explained that I was a Shabbat observer; therefore, it was forbidden for me to write on that day. I don't think he understood my explanation, but he did not seem bothered by it. As I recall, he was a partner in the firm's San Francisco office, and if New York hired me, that was okay with him. Victory for me. To fully appreciate the extent of this victory, it is important to note that these large firms only started hiring Jews, and certainly not Shabbat-observing Jews, in the early 1950s.

A few weeks after my return from Chicago, I was given an assignment that required me to be in the office on Saturday. When I said I could not come in the next day, the personnel director asked, "What is the difference between watching football and working on Saturday?" When I told him that I would not be watching football and further explained how we observed the Shabbat, he quickly found someone else to work on the assignment.

Somehow, I avoided any additional conflicts until Good Friday 1969, which coincided with the first day of Passover. A day before the holiday, my non-Jewish supervisor gave me a list of things that had to be completed on Friday. When I explained that I would not be working on Friday, he said that I had to come in because he had tickets to take his daughter to the circus at Madison Square Garden and there was work that needed to be completed that day. He was not happy when I told him I was still not going to work on Friday, and his anger remained when he wrote my performance evaluation several months later. For the most part, I avoided future conflicts by working many Sundays to make up for the lost hours of not working on Saturdays. Despite my willingness to work the same number of hours in five-and-a-half days that everyone else was working in six days, it was difficult not to feel eyes staring at me when I left early on Fridays. However, there were occasions when leaving early on Friday, despite the stares, had its rewards.

I shared an office with a Jewish lawyer named Stan Hammerman, and one Friday, as I was getting ready to leave early, Stan told me that his grandfather, who was Shabbat observant, always told him to be *shomer Shabbat*. Stan said he always dismissed his grandfather's request as the rumblings of an old-fashioned Jew who still thought he was in the old country, but, when he saw how relaxed I was on Friday because despite whatever unreasonable workload was assigned to me I could put everything from the office out of my mind and enjoy a relaxing, spiritual Shabbat with my family, he began to think that maybe his grandfather wasn't so old fashioned after all. Unfortunately, while I was successful in convincing him of the beauty of Shabbat, I was not successful in turning him into a Shabbat observer.

While leaving early on Friday and substituting Sundays in place of Saturdays was workable, the issue of the Jewish holidays, especially Passover (which often coincided with the deadline for filing taxes — the busiest time of the year), was another matter. If Passover began in the middle of the week, I needed to take off four days at the busiest time of the year. Of course, I utilized vacation days for holidays, but taking a vacation week during the middle of tax filing season was unheard of. Furthermore, I found out that while some (but certainly not a majority) of my Jewish supervisors took time off work for Rosh Hashanah and Yom Kippur, they had no idea about Passover (other than the Seder, which is the service and meal of the first evening of Passover to commemorate the Jews' exodus from Egypt). They had never even heard of the other Jewish holidays, Sukkot and Shavuot.

I anxiously looked at the Hebrew calendar as soon as it came in the mail during the summer, praying that most of the holidays would be on Saturdays and Sundays. That I was a "maverick" at Arthur Andersen and was willing to undertake the challenge of opening these large firms to a person who was *shomer Shabbat* is not surprising considering the example set by my mother, Ruth Miller, *a"h*.

When I was in high school, my mother took a job as a secretary at the Metropolitan Life Insurance Company home office. Although the head office was huge, Mom always thought that she was the only *shomer Shabbat* employee. As an excellent worker, she had to resist the pleas of her supervisors to become a full-time employee. She continued to end her day at 3:25 p.m. so that she would be home prior to the onset of Shabbat.

Mom had been working at the Met for less than a year when Yom Kippur fell on a Wednesday. My mother informed Mary Margaret, her immediate superior, that she would be taking Wednesday off from work. Mary Margaret told her that if she didn't come in on Wednesday, she should not bother to come in on Thursday. With that threat, my mother started cleaning out her desk. When the head of her department came over and asked her what she was doing, she explained what had happened and said that since she couldn't work on Wednesday, she assumed she had just been fired and was leaving.

The head of the department told her not to worry; she could take the day off and come back to work on Thursday. When my mother came home the evening prior to Yom Kippur, she was still so furious at Mary Margaret that when she related the incident to us, she said that she hoped Mary Margaret broke her leg. While we were having dinner on the Thursday after Yom Kippur, my father asked her what, if anything, Mary Margaret said when Mom had arrived at work. My mom responded: "Mary Margaret wasn't in today. She fell yesterday and broke her leg." That story stayed with me for so many years that when I delivered a eulogy following my mother's passing in December 1994, I had to share it.

With that upbringing as my inspiration, fighting for the right of a person to be *shomer Shabbat* was not difficult for me. Eventually, the large accounting and law firms accepted more and more *shomer Shabbat* employees, and the firms adjusted to the work schedule of these employees who were just too good at their jobs not to be tolerated for their religious beliefs.

There were several incidents in which I take great pride, and they made the difficulties that I endured in standing up for my rights worthwhile. The first incident occurred in 1968, when my firm was scheduling its holiday party at the Waldorf Astoria Hotel in New York.

When I received the invitation, I went to personnel and asked them to order kosher food for Ronnie and me. A few weeks went by before I received a call from the Waldorf's banquet manager saying that no one at the Waldorf had any idea what kosher food was or where to get it. He requested that I purchase the kosher meals and said that I would be reimbursed for the cost.

By 1975, we had a kosher table and the hotel knew where to get and how to serve kosher meals. Unfortunately, when Ronnie and I arrived at the hotel, someone from the banquet department said that the *mashgiach* (supervisor of the standards of kosher food) had locked our meals in the refrigerator before he went home. Anticipating eating carrots for the evening, we were reassured when the banquet manager told us that they had obtained kosher food from a nearby hospital. When we received our meals, we were somewhat disappointed to discover that the hospital had sent over meals intended for someone who was on a salt-free, sugar-free diet. I think we would have enjoyed the carrots more than the meals.

The second incident occurred in 1984. At the time, I was partner-in-charge of the tax department in Worcester, Massachusetts. I had been transferred there in 1978. The incident occurred when I was teaching at a firm tax seminar in Houston, Texas. During the afternoon break, one of the young lawyers from the New York office approached me very carefully, clearly concerned that he was daring to approach a partner in the firm. Noticing his hesitation to speak to me, I asked him what I could do for him, and he replied, "Is it okay if I ask you a personal question?"

"Please, ask away," I said, not having any idea what was on his mind.

"I heard that you were *shomer Shabbat*?"

When I nodded in the affirmative, he told me that one of the students was saying *Kaddish* (a Jewish prayer for the deceased), and they needed me to make up the required number of ten men for the prayer to be said. Needless to say, it was one of the most satisfying prayer services I had ever attended.

Shortly thereafter, I was working in the New York office and observed that there were seven members of the tax department all eating lunch together, all wearing *yarmulkes* (skullcaps worn by Jewish men). I went over to one of my New York partners who had played a major role in protecting me from others who were not as sympathetic to my religious beliefs as they could have been and asked, "Do these kids have any idea what it was like for me when I first started, making up the rules of the workplace as they applied to someone who was *shomer Shabbat* on an as-needed basis?" "Not really," he replied. "But I did hear someone refer to you as 'the Jackie Robinson of the *shomer Shabbat* professionals.'" I went back to Worcester with a big smile on my face.

The final incident occurred after I was promoted to partner-in-charge of the tax department when our firm, KMG, merged with Peat Marwick, the world's largest public service firm. I received a memo from the National Office in Washington reminding me that as partner-in-charge, I was required to attend a special tax meeting in October. I looked at my calendar and noticed that the meeting conflicted with the first two days of Sukkot (a Jewish festival that occurs in the fall and celebrates God's protection of the Jews in the wilderness during biblical times). I responded that I would not be able to attend as I had a conflicting engagement. The partner responsible for the meeting called up the partner-in-charge of the Worcester office and told him that my attendance was mandatory; no excuses would be accepted. When the partner-in-charge told him that I had a religious holiday that coincided with the conference, the meeting coordinator, who was himself Jewish, told my partner-in-charge that I must have been lying, as he had scheduled the meeting for after the Jewish Holidays. He then called me to find out "what I was trying to pull," as, according to him, the holidays were in September. I told him that I wasn't talking about Rosh Hashanah or Yom Kippur. I was referring to Sukkot. I received an apology for the scheduling conflict, an official excused absence from the meeting, and assurance that in future years the meeting would be scheduled for after Sukkot. What a long way from where I had started in 1968!

Despite all of the incredible progress I made over the years, I could not have reached the level that I did (including partner-in-charge of the tax department of the Worcester office, member of the firm's tax advisory board, and a frequent teacher at tax seminars all over the country) without the help and assistance of many individuals, almost all of whom were Jewish and were determined to ensure that I was evaluated solely on my merit and not on my different work habits.

One individual deserves special praise in this regard because he was not Jewish: Richard Nelowet, who was partner-in-charge of my division at Arthur Andersen. In January 1972, after some difficulties I had with one of the partners concerning my leaving a client meeting early on a Friday, I decided that I'd had enough. I was hired by a medium-sized firm with a reputation for welcoming *shomer Shabbat* employees, and I proceeded to hand in my resignation to Mr. Nelowet. When he asked me why I was leaving, I explained the difficulties that I frequently encountered due to my religious observances. Mr. Nelowet said that if that was my decision, so be it, but he wanted me to consider one important fact. He told me that I was well liked by most of the partners and that I was scheduled for promotion. "If," he continued, "you feel you have to leave because of religious issues, then you will be making it more difficult for the firm to hire more *shomer Shabbat* employees." After thinking about it over the weekend, I decided that if I left the firm for religious reasons, I would be doing a disservice to those who followed in my footsteps. I stayed for another year, and then I left the firm for completely different reasons.

Another incident that I love to recount occurred with my secretary in New York. She was not Jewish, but she was very sensitive to my religious needs. On Fridays in the winter months, I always left the office between 2 and 2:30 p.m. so that I could return to my Brooklyn home prior to the onset of Shabbat. Once New York entered daylight savings time, however, there was no need for me to leave that early, and I usually left around 4 p.m. or later. So, one Friday afternoon, there I was plugging away at my desk when the clock said it was 3 p.m. My secretary walked into my office, hands on her hips, with a scowl on her face. When I asked her what was wrong, she asked, "Do you know what time it is?!" I suddenly realized that my secretary was unaware of the rules of the onset of Shabbat and just assumed that the magic time for departure was between 2 and 2:30 p.m. I could either try and explain the rules to her, including the effect that the switch to daylight savings time had on the time I needed to leave, or I could just thank her for reminding me. I promptly thanked her and left the office much earlier than I needed to. I continued to leave by 2:30 p.m. every Friday afternoon until I transferred to Worcester in 1978.

Another incident happened after I had been transferred to the office in Worcester, Massachusetts. My secretary, Bess, who was Greek and thought the geographical proximity of Greece to Israel made us almost related, took an immediate liking to me as the only Jewish employee in the office. Bess knew that I kept a Jewish calendar in my desk drawer so that I would know the dates of the Jewish holidays and would not schedule a meeting or seminar (usually months in advance) for the same day as a Jewish holiday. All I needed to do was open my desk, see when Shavuot was, and make sure my schedule was okay. Bess would also look at my calendar so that she knew when the holidays were. She never failed to send me a Hallmark card for an upcoming holiday—Purim, Chanukah, Passover…. I could always count on a card being sent to my house. One year, knowing that I was not coming into work because of a holiday, she went to my calendar, looked at what it said, and, since she couldn't find an appropriate card, left a big note on my desk wishing me "Happy Yizkor."

- 5 -

IN THE BEGINNING

WHILE ALL THIS WAS GOING on in my professional life, I still was a member of the JDL. Although I was content that I had paid my dues, I was not active in any JDL activities, and I cannot recall ever attending any of their rallies. On the other hand, Rabbi Kahane and the JDL were by no means inactive. By 1969, the JDL's self-described purpose was to protect Jews from local manifestations of anti-Semitism. Every Halloween, JDL members patrolled Jewish cemeteries to prevent the annual desecration of graves associated with Halloween. On Election Day, JDL members escorted elderly Jews who lived in poorer neighborhoods in New York to the polls so that they could cast their ballots and return home in safety. JDL members patrolled mixed neighborhoods, providing additional security to elderly Jews walking home from evening prayer services. Security issues were of major importance, as these years saw the mass exodus of New York's Jewish population into the suburbs, leaving the poor and elderly behind to become victims of violent crimes in the racially and ethnically changing neighborhoods.

Several years later, after I became more involved in the JDL, I joined JDL civilian patrols in the Boro Park section of Brooklyn. There had been a rash of muggings of elderly Jews who were coming home from evening prayer services, and the police could do little to prevent these random attacks. The JDL provided security by driving a car with five or six JDL members (I was a driver on several occasions) closely and slowly behind a JDL member who was dressed as an elderly, defenseless Jew on his way home. This JDL member walked up and down the streets of Boro Park with a car trailing at a safe distance but never more than a few seconds away. If the seemingly elderly man was accosted, the trailing car quickly pulled alongside the JDL member, and, if he was being attacked, the other JDL members intervened (as a lawyer, I stayed in the car). In some cases, the JDL members got very physical with the assailants and taught them not to mess with the Jews of Boro Park. After a few weeks of these patrols, word got around Boro Park of the so-called Jewish vigilantes and the streets became safe again.

My lack of involvement in any of these activities during their early years was not the result of any disagreement I had with them. I just did not have the time. I worked between 60 and 80 hours a week in the tax department of Arthur Andersen, and I attended the graduate tax program at New York University School of Law twice a week to pursue a Masters in Law, specializing in taxation. My wife always liked the two nights a week that I went to class, as I came home at 10:30 p.m., which Ronnie referred to as my "early nights." As such, any free time that I had was spent with my family.

Besides providing security for elderly Jews in marginal neighborhoods, by 1969, the JDL had become extremely controversial, as its activities included taking on the Soviet Union by making the issue of freedom for Soviet Jews its top priority. Suddenly, what had first seemed to be pranks began increasing in severity. Whether it was at a performance of the Moscow ballet, the Russian opera, a Russian circus, or any other performance involving Russian performers, the show was disrupted by JDL members. At first, bags of marbles were set loose to roll down the aisles of the Lincoln Center, Carnegie Hall, or whatever venue was hosting the Russian performance. From marbles, the distractions graduated to smoke bombs and other nuisances designed to frustrate the audience but guaranteed to make the late-night news. After a description of such a performance disruption, the TV reporter always aired a statement by a JDL spokesperson to the effect that there could be no détente with the Soviet Union until Jews were free to emigrate to Israel.

With these nightly demands for freedom for Russian Jews made by Rabbi Kahane, the issue was adopted by all mainstream Jewish organizations, which is exactly what Rabbi Kahane wanted to happen. As the disruption of Soviet performances increased, Soviet complaints to the State Department also increased, thereby putting pressure on the New York City Police to arrest the individuals who were caught perpetrating these acts. Nevertheless, as a result of these seemingly childish nuisance-type acts, everyone seemed to be talking about the issue of Soviet Jewry. The cry of "Let My People Go" became part of our everyday vocabulary.

Despite all this, mainstream Jewish leaders, including prominent rabbis, believed that these activities were "un-Jewish." They did not support these young people who were risking their freedom to raise awareness about the concerns of Soviet Jews among the masses, and they condemned both Rabbi Kahane and the JDL's activities. When discussing the JDL's behavior among friends, I generally expressed my support for Rabbi Kahane and the JDL. However, I was not overly vocal in these discussions. I especially avoided arguing with those who did not approve of the JDL's actions.

By 1970, JDL members were regularly harassing Soviet diplomats and their families as they walked in the neighborhood of the Soviet Mission near the United Nations on 67th Street on Manhattan's Upper East Side. Additionally, demonstrations near the Mission were designed to make life uncomfortable for the Russians. For example, in May 1970, 50 JDL members entered the Park East Synagogue, situated across the street from the Soviet Mission. From the roof and scaffolding on the building, they hung banners protesting the treatment of Soviet Jews. To the background of martial music played from the synagogue's roof, JDL members, using loudspeakers, shouted their demands to free Soviet Jews. The synagogue takeover lasted several hours, even after the synagogue's rabbi pleaded with Rabbi Kahane to end the protest. In November 1970, the JDL once again used the proximity of the Park East Synagogue to hold an anti-Soviet demonstration. Unlike the first takeover in May, this time, the police were called in to end the takeover.

Even after a court order prevented any demonstrations within 500 yards of the Mission, the JDL harassed diplomats and their families as they went about their activities of daily life, such as doing their shopping, walking to the subway, taking their children to school, etc. The intensity of these anti-Soviet activities increased, and after each incident, Rabbi Kahane publicly stated that the Russians would not be free in New York until Russian Jews were freed. Eventually, these activities against Russian interests in the United States increased in scope and could no longer be ignored by the Soviet Union.

By the summer of 1970, the Soviet government demanded better protection for its citizens, thereby further increasing the JDL's publicity, which Rabbi Kahane was determined to use to raise awareness of the treatment of Soviet Jews among mainstream Jewish leaders. What started out as nuisance-type activities, like rolling marbles on the floor of a concert, quickly accelerated into much more serious activities, including shootings at Russian facilities, fire bombings, and other serious offenses.

At the same time, the JDL organized a boycott of companies that were doing business with the Soviet Union. The JDL set up a telephone hotline informing callers of which consumer products should be boycotted. The most famous name on the list was Pepsi Cola, which was on sale in the Soviet Union. JDL members pasted thousands of stickers proclaiming "Pepsi Kills" on store windows and telephone booths and in subway cars all over the city.

While I had little difficulty with the nuisance activities, I admit that I was not comfortable with random shootings and other violent acts. Regardless of how I felt and what my personal beliefs were, I was totally divorced from any of these activities, content that I had paid dues to the JDL during the Ocean Brownsville crises but had no further contact with or participation in anything associated with the JDL. Quite simply, I had my family life and career, which consumed most of my time.

All that changed one night with a single phone call.

- 6 -

WE NEED YOUR HELP

L ATE ONE EVENING IN 1971, I received a call from someone named Bob Persky who said he was calling from the JDL.

"Do I need to pay my dues again? I inquired of Mr. Persky.

"I am not calling about dues. I am a lawyer, and I was going through the JDL membership files looking for other lawyers and came across your membership application. I need your help."

Mr. Persky went on to explain that with the expansion of JDL's activities, literally dozens of teenagers were being arrested on a weekly basis, and they were expecting the JDL to provide them with a lawyer when they appeared in court. Mr. Persky was calling to see if I could be of assistance in providing legal representation to these JDL members. I quickly explained that I was not a criminal attorney, as my practice was limited to tax issues. Furthermore, I was not even affiliated with a law firm, as I was working for one of the Big Eight accounting firms. So, I really couldn't be of any help to him. Ignoring my excuse, Bob went on to explain the problem, and it literally changed my life.

Bob was the only lawyer who was appearing on behalf of the arrested JDL members. The sheer volume of cases, even cases that required little or no time to dispose of, was overwhelming. To make matters even more difficult, most of the arrests took place in the evening, so the JDL members were often required to appear at Manhattan's Night Court (a part of the criminal justice system that processed arrests during the evening, usually during the "graveyard shift," which ran from 1 to 9 a.m.). Therefore, Persky was suffering from sleep deprivation.

The most pressing matter, however, was the fact that Persky lived and practiced law in New Jersey and was not admitted to practice law in New York. In order for a lawyer to appear in any court, he must be admitted to practice law in that jurisdiction. So, when I passed the New York State Bar Examination and was admitted to practice in New York in 1968, I was permitted to represent clients in the New York State court system. Separate admissions were required to represent clients in the federal courts for the New York federal districts. I was not permitted to appear in court in any of the other 49 states nor in any of the other federal district courts unless I made a motion to be admitted to practice in a particular jurisdiction for a particular case. As Bob Persky had only been admitted to practice in New Jersey, each time he appeared in a New York court, he had to make a motion to be admitted to practice for the day so that he could represent the JDL kids.

Except in unusual circumstances, the Assistant District Attorney (ADA) will not object, and the judge will grant the motion admitting the lawyer to appear in court for the day. However, because JDL activities against Russian interests in the United States had increased and pressure was being exerted in diplomatic circles, the ADA objected to Mr. Persky's admittance in one New York case and indicated that he had been instructed by his superiors to do so.

"What has all this got to do with me?" I inquired.

Mr. Persky reiterated that no other lawyers (besides for himself) were involved in these cases, and he needed someone to appear with him and be the attorney of record. In that way, he could appear as my associate and represent the JDL kids even though I was the one admitted to practice law in New York.

"But I wouldn't know what to do. I do not practice criminal law. I don't practice any law besides tax law."

WE NEED YOUR HELP

Mr. Persky assured me that all I had to do was appear with him in court, and, after I made an appearance as defense counsel, he would take over. He further assured me that these cases were usually disposed of quickly, and if all went well, we would be finished by 3 a.m., so, as I was still living on the Lower East Side, I would be home by 3:30 a.m. I continued to protest, but Mr. Persky was very convincing. I could not believe him when he said, "No other lawyers besides the two of us are available." Apparently, even lawyers who were sympathetic to the JDL's activities were not interested in frequent night calls or the volume of calls requiring a daytime presence for a nonpaying client. Besides, these arraignments were not an occasional event. The JDL was active almost every night, so a lawyer could be in court several times a week.

Mr. Persky said if I did not assist him, and if he were barred from practicing in New York, the JDL kids would not have any legal representation. He made it clear that the kids had sworn not to be represented by means of legal aid, as they were of the belief that the Jewish community owed them legal representation. Persky then told me, "The Jewish community's representation consists of Robert Persky of Jersey City, New Jersey, and, if you agree, Arthur Miller of the Lower East Side." Growing up in a home where concern for our fellow Jews was of paramount importance, I could not refuse. Thus, my life changed dramatically for the next few years.

- 7 -

GETTING MY FEET WET

IT SEEMED LIKE THE ARRESTS of JDL members increased as soon as I agreed to help. Before I knew it, late-night phone calls had become part of my regular routine.

Already coming home quite late at night from work, there were times that I had to go to Night Court after I finished dinner. On those occasions when the arraignment was put off until the morning, I had to appear in court before I went to my office. Spending an hour or two in court meant that I needed to stay even later in my office.

As a true neophyte, I met Bob Persky outside the courtroom, entered my notice of appearance, and then turned things over to Bob. The process was quite simple. Before I knew it, I was representing JDL members in court by myself. I quickly learned the magic words, requesting that the judge consider granting the offending youths an "ACD." In criminal procedure, an adjournment in contemplation of dismissal (ACD or ACOD) allows a court to defer the disposition of a defendant's case. It carries the potential that the defendant's charge will be dismissed and the record of the arrest erased from public records — if the defendant does not engage in additional criminal conduct or other acts prohibited by the court.

In accordance with this procedure, when first-time juvenile protesters were arrested, I requested an ACD, the judge adjourned any action on the matter, and, if the young man was not rearrested within a six-month period, the charges would be dismissed. Of even greater importance is the fact that if the charges were dismissed, the individual could later answer college questionnaires and future employment applications stating that he had never been arrested.

At first, most of the cases Persky let me handle on my own were first timers, so I was successful in obtaining ACDs. I felt quite confident until the day I requested an ACD and the ADA prosecuting the case objected. This was the third time the individual had been arrested, clearly violating the prior terms of his adjournment. I was not prepared for this development and was about to call for help when Persky arrived in court. Persky then informed me that the judge assigned to the case was Judge Bruce Wright, so I should continue with the case. I had to admit that I had never heard of Judge Bruce Wright, but I soon learned that he was a blessing from God.

In reality, Judge Wright was a righteous non-Jew, although there was no such award in the New York City Criminal Justice Division. Judge Wright was an African American who had battled against discrimination most of his young life. Despite this discrimination, he had become a lawyer and had been appointed to the Supreme Court of New York (despite its name as "Supreme," the court is one of the lower courts in the New York State Judicial Branch). In 1970, he had been assigned to the criminal courts. Judge Wright believed that Jewish youths had the responsibility to fight for Soviet Jews in their battle against the Soviet government. Accordingly, he worked behind the scenes to have JDL cases assigned to his court, where he was most lenient in finding grounds for dismissing the charges. There were times when Judge Wright, while listening to the news at home, heard about the arrest of JDL members who were scheduled to be arraigned at Night Court and then left his home to replace the Night Court judge so that he could handle the cases. For his actions in most cases involving minorities, including JDL cases, he earned the nickname of "Turn 'Em Loose, Bruce."

Only later did I discover that while defendants considered this title a badge of honor, in reality, the nickname had been given to him by the police in protest against his liberal bail and sentencing rulings. When Judge Wright was criticized for his liberal bail policies, he deflected these criticisms with a reminder that both the United States Constitution and the New York Constitution prohibited excessive bail. In explaining his concept of excessive bail, Judge Wright stated that to a defendant who does not have a penny to his name, a bail of two cents is excessive. I appeared before him many times, and he made me feel like a hero for handling these cases. Judge Wright served as a judge for over 25 years, and I was saddened when I read that he passed away in 2005. In 2013, the name of a street in Harlem was changed to "Judge Bruce Wright Place," a fitting tribute to a heroic man.

- 8 -

THINGS BEGIN TO HEAT UP

A T FIRST, MY COURT APPEARANCES went according to plan. Almost all of my early court appearances involved requesting ACDs, which the judge granted. I would then advise my young client to stay out of trouble for the few months that the judge had stated in the adjournment. Occasionally, the ADA would object, and I would have to convince the judge to grant the ACD. My usual explanation to the judge was that the young JDL member was an excellent student and an arrest record could hamper his ability to be accepted into an Ivy League school. The judge usually accepted these requests with an admonishment to the JDL member that if he violated the terms of his ACD, he should not expect leniency, and he would indeed have a criminal record and might even spend some time in jail.

I felt very good about myself for two reasons. The first reason was that my criminal court appearances were a nice change of pace from my tax practice, as I was appearing in a courtroom setting. The second reason was that I really felt like I was accomplishing something for Soviet Jewry, and I believed that the JDL's actions, while keeping the issue of Russian Jewry in the news, didn't really harm anyone.

However, it didn't take long for Rabbi Kahane and the JDL to increase the scope and severity of their activities. At first, the harassment of Soviet diplomats and their families angered the Russians, who complained forcefully to the State Department. As explained in the previous chapter, the JDL had identified the families of diplomats and began harassing their wives and children in their everyday activities. The Russians also owned a very large enclave in Glen Cove, an exclusive neighborhood on Long Island. The residents of Glen Cove did not take kindly to young Jews parading through their town harassing Russian diplomats and their families. Eventually, the Soviet Mission to the United Nations became off-limits to the JDL, as the Mission obtained a restraining order preventing the JDL from coming within 500 yards of its building.

JDL harassment interfered with attempts by the United States and Russia to increase economic cooperation, as the Russians needed American grain to help feed their population. However, all of these activities paled in comparison to what was soon to come. On April 22, 1971, a bomb in an attaché case exploded at the offices of the Amtorg Trading Corporation, the Soviet trade agency, on Lexington Avenue. Although no one was injured in the blast, the premises were badly damaged. As expected, the Soviets were furious and demanded that the Americans find those who were responsible. Several people had called the press prior to the bomb explosion demanding freedom for Soviet Jewry, thereby bringing the JDL into the spotlight as the responsible party.

Shortly thereafter, I started to receive calls from JDL members advising me that they had been ordered to appear before a grand jury investigating these more violent activities and that they wanted me to be present when they were in the grand jury room. In addition to grand jury appearances, JDL members had been ordered to appear before Assistant United States Attorneys and agents of the FBI, who were questioning the JDL members about their possible participation in or what they knew about the Amtorg bombing. No matter how busy I was at work, I cannot recall one instance in which I did not make myself available to provide whatever assistance I could to the JDL members. While working between 10 and 14 hours a day at my office, I often left the office in the middle of the afternoon to meet my JDL "clients" either at the courthouse or at the FBI offices.

- 9 -

MY FIRST TRIAL

DESPITE BOB PERSKY'S ASSURANCES THAT I would only have to appear at arraignments, as I earned a reputation for always making myself available to appear in court, it was only a matter of time before I was asked to appear in court in a trial.

There was a program at Brooklyn College in 1972 concerning Israeli–Palestinian issues. The program was not peaceful, as Jewish students and Palestinian supporters got into a boisterous shouting and shoving match. At some point during the demonstration, an Arab supporter named Mustafa was punched in the face and received several facial injuries. Despite the fact that Mustafa was not a student at the college, the college authorities cooperated with Mustafa in attempting to find out who had punched him. Accordingly, they provided Mustafa with photographs from the demonstration taken by a photographer for the school newspaper. Mustafa looked at the pictures and identified a Jewish student leader named Josh as the culprit. The police then arrested Josh, and he was charged with assault and related charges. As an honors student with no previous record, Josh pleaded not guilty and was released without bail.

Although he was not a JDL member, Josh asked some JDL members for the name of a lawyer who could represent him at his trial. Someone recommended me, and Josh called me one evening to see if I would represent him. I met with Josh and his parents in their home in the Crown Heights section of Brooklyn. During our meeting, Josh insisted that he did not throw the punch that hit Mustafa. Josh further told me that a college dean who was at the demonstration was willing to testify that Josh was with him as an observer the entire time. After speaking to the dean, I thought that this would be an appropriate case for me tackle as my first trial, so I agreed to take the case.

I knew that the police's method of showing the photographs to Mustafa raised some questions about the admissibility of Mustafa's identification of Josh as the one who hit him. Nevertheless, I did not bring a motion to suppress the evidence, as I was concerned that such a motion was beyond my limited capabilities. I waited anxiously for the trial date. The trial started, and the ADA trying the case for the prosecution questioned Mustafa about the demonstration, the extent of his injuries, and more. When Mustafa finished his testimony, the ADA announced, "the People rest." At no time during his testimony did he testify concerning who had hit him. As I listened to his testimony and prepared a vigorous cross-examination, visions of Perry Mason went through my head.

When Mustafa finished his testimony, I already knew I would win the case. When the judge asked me what I wanted to do, I told him I wanted to cross-examine the witness. The judge told me that if that was what I wanted to do, that was fine, but he must have realized my inexperience. He said, "You can cross-examine the witness, but I would look quite favorably on a motion to dismiss the charges for failure to prove a prima facie case. In fact, if such a motion was made, we could all adjourn for an early lunch." Failure to prove a prima facie case occurs when, as a matter of law, if all of the evidence presented by the prosecution is deemed to be true, the facts are insufficient to support a guilty verdict, so the charges are dismissed without the need to present any defense.

Although I really wanted to conduct my very first cross-examination, I was smart enough to realize that the judge was telling me what to do, as there was no case against Josh. Thus, I made a motion for dismissal. The judge granted my motion, and Josh was free. Recognizing that the trial was over, Mustafa began to leave the courtroom. When the judge asked him where he was going, Mustafa, confused, said he was going home. "Just a minute," said the judge. "I have before me a sworn complaint signed by you saying that the defendant was the one who punched you. As you gave no testimony to that effect at this trial, I have no choice but to assume you perjured yourself when you signed the complaint. Accordingly, I am instructing the bailiff to take you into custody, and the district attorney should charge you with perjury." As Mustafa was handcuffed and led away, we were overcome with joy. Justice had been done. More importantly, I was undefeated. I had a perfect 1–0 record.

- 10 -

MY SECOND TRIAL

S EVERAL MONTHS LATER, I RECEIVED a call from someone named Sam. Sam needed a lawyer, as he had been arrested and was awaiting trial. He explained that there had been a demonstration at the United Nations building and that the Tactical Patrol Force (TPF) had eventually been called in to break up the demonstration.

I later learned that the police usually permitted these demonstrations for a period of time, after which a police captain would come over to me (I always introduced myself as a lawyer for the demonstrators) and tell me it was time to end the demonstration. I would then announce to the demonstrators that anyone who did not want to get arrested should leave. More often than not, the demonstrators refused to end their protest, insisting on being arrested, thereby increasing coverage of the event in the news. Photos or video recordings of the police picking up the demonstrators who were sitting in the street and refused to move made for good copy on the TV news or in the paper.

One time, my wife, wheeling our daughter, Aliza, in a stroller, attended a demonstration and sat down in the street with the other demonstrators. One of the police officers who was at the demonstration came over to me and said, "Arthur, we are going to start arresting demonstrators. Do you really want your wife and daughter to be hauled off in a paddy wagon and brought to the local police station? Do yourself a favor and tell your wife to leave the demonstration." I thanked him for his advice, and Ronnie and Aliza adjourned to the sidewalk.

I was not present at the demonstration when Sam was arrested, and I found out that this particular demonstration did not end peacefully. The demonstrators refused to leave the environs of the United Nations building, and the police could not get them to move. As a result, the police called in the TPF. The TPF was a specially trained unit of the police formed in 1959 to deal with rising crime in New York. With special training in crowd control, the TPF members, who were all well over 6 ft tall and trained in martial arts, were assigned to break up the JDL demonstrations that were offensive to the Soviet diplomats.

At the demonstration in question, Sam, who was of stocky build and no more than 5 ½ ft tall, was arrested for resisting arrest and assaulting a TPF officer. Sam pleaded not guilty and then contacted me and asked if I would defend him at his trial. When we spoke on the telephone, my first concern was to see if I could obtain an ACD. I was concerned that the trial would come down to Sam's word against a decorated member of the TPF. Sam told me, however, that he had been arrested on more than one occasion and an ACD had not been granted at his arraignment. A trial date had been set.

I then met Sam for the first time. He had a photograph from the *New York Post* showing a helmeted TPF officer, who was at least 6 ft 4 in tall, with his nightstick around Sam's throat. It was hard for me to believe that anyone of Sam's size would assault a TPF officer who was helmeted, armed with a nightstick, and specially trained. With the photograph as my only physical evidence, I agreed to try the case. At trial I selected, without too much opposition from the ADA, what appeared to be a majority of elderly Jewish mothers for the jury.

After the TPF officer testified, I cross-examined him about the photograph, inquiring as to who was assaulting whom. I never called Sam to the stand and rested my case after the cross-examination. On summation, I asked the jury to review the photograph and ask themselves if they really believed that Sam could assault this officer, who literally towered over him and was apparently choking him with his nightstick. It took the jury less than 20 minutes for the jury to return with a verdict of not guilty. As I was now 2–0, I felt very good about myself. Then, Sam turned to me and said, "I appreciate your defense, but I want you to know I could have taken the TPF officer any time." Several months later, I had another occasion on which I needed to assist Sam — in what I call "The Erev Shabbat Case."

- 11 -

THE EREV SHABBAT CASE

O N A FRIDAY EVENING IN June, around ten minutes before Shabbat, I received a call from Sam, who needed my help in a matter that was very pressing.

Sam explained that he had been a witness in criminal court that morning and that the judge had called a recess for the summer weekend. When he did so, the judge reminded Sam that he was required to return to court at 9:30 a.m. on Monday morning in order to continue his testimony. Sam called me to say that more than 20 police officers had surrounded his house, which was located in a predominately Jewish neighborhood in Brooklyn. One officer, a lieutenant, had entered his house and sought to take Sam into custody in order to ensure his appearance on Monday. There was no basis for taking him into custody, as the judge had dismissed him Friday morning without issuing a subpoena to ensure his return. For his part, Sam, despite his many appearances in court, had never missed a scheduled appearance. To make matters worse, the lieutenant told Sam that he had until 8:00 p.m. to leave with the lieutenant, or he would be forcefully removed from the premises.

It was clear to me that the police contingent, having arrived at Sam's house at 7:15 p.m., were intent on waiting until the exact moment that Shabbat would begin before arresting Sam. Sam then told me that his family were ultra-orthodox and that it would destroy his father if the police arrested him and drove him away on Shabbat in full view of his many orthodox neighbors. I asked Sam to put the lieutenant on the phone. I obtained his name and badge number and asked him if he could respect the prohibition against Sam riding in a car on Shabbat with my assurance that I would bring him to court on Monday morning. The lieutenant told me that he "was only following orders," and he had to bring Sam in at 8:00 p.m.

After telling the lieutenant that "just following orders" did not work at Nuremberg, I informed him that I did not think it would protect him, the Police Department, or the City of New York in the civil rights lawsuit I intended to bring if he proceeded to force Sam to violate Shabbat. In so doing, I assumed that the lieutenant would not know that this was an idle threat, as bringing such a lawsuit was beyond my capabilities at this time. Then, I hung up the phone. I had no idea what to do next or even if I was allowed to do anything more, as my wife had already lit candles (from which time, it is prohibited to undertake any non-Shabbat activities), and I knew it was too late to call my rabbi to ask whether keeping a religious Jew from being arrested was an activity that I could do after Shabbat had already begun.

A few years later, I was in a somewhat similar situation when my family and I were in a bungalow colony in the Catskills. Late one Friday night, my neighbor got into a shouting match with the owner of the colony, eventually leading to the local police being called and my neighbor being arrested. When the police said that she would be brought before the judge at the police station and would probably remain in jail until Monday morning, I quickly asked a rabbi (who was part of the crowd that had gathered during the commotion) what I was allowed to do to get her released that night. The rabbi said that there was no problem with me walking to the police station and seeking her release that night. The police agreed to delay bringing my neighbor before the judge until I was able to walk to the station (my neighbor was placed in the police car and was driven to the station). As long as I was not going to be paid for going to the police station (I was not), I would not technically be working on Shabbat; therefore, I could go to the police station and legally represent my neighbor. The judge was most sympathetic to my request that she be released, and I promised to make sure that she behaved herself and did not get into another incident with the owner upon her return to the bungalow colony. Thanking him, we proceeded to walk back to the bungalow colony, where we arrived at around 3:00 a.m.

Sam's case was much different because it appeared that I might need to do certain activities, like making phone calls, after Shabbat had begun. My objective was not, as in the bungalow case, to get Sam released after he had been arrested. My goal was to prevent the arrest itself. Not knowing what else to do and still within the 18-minute window from the time the candles were lit until the actual onset of Shabbat, I called the judge's chambers, fully aware that it was unlikely the judge would be in his chambers late Friday evening in the summer. Much to my surprise, the phone was answered on the first ring, and it was the Honorable Jack Weinstein who answered. I apologized profusely for calling him at the late hour, related what was transpiring at Sam's residence, and explained my dilemma, including telling him that I was probably in violation of the Shabbat, but I did not know what else to do.

Expecting to face the wrath of the judge for my unusual actions, I was thrilled when he was, instead, furious at the police for attempting to bring Sam into custody when he had let Sam go home with just a verbal order for him to return on Monday. The judge asked me for Sam's phone number and said he would take care of the matter. He wished me a pleasant Shabbat. After Shabbat was over, I called Sam. He told me that the judge had called, spoken with the lieutenant, must have threatened him with charges of contempt of court, and ordered him to leave the premises. I was overjoyed at what I had accomplished.

When Sam told all of his JDL friends what his lawyer had done, my caseload seemed to increase almost immediately. Too bad I was working pro bono, or I might have made some serious money.

- 12 -

THANK YOU, JOE COLOMBO

IT WAS NEARING MIDNIGHT ON a Saturday evening, and I was home watching a sporting event on TV when I received a call from a JDL member who was at the police station on Avenue U in Brooklyn, not far from my home on Avenue R.

As the story unfolded, I learned that there had been a dance at the Kingsway Jewish Center on Kings Highway. During the evening, a group of youths of Italian descent attempted on several occasions to crash the dance. The Jewish teenagers at the dance locked the doors to keep the non-Jewish kids out of the Jewish Center, but problems started to develop when the Jewish teenagers wanted to leave the premises. The Center repeatedly called 911, requesting help from the police so that the Jewish kids could leave without being harassed by the Italian kids. However, Saturday night was a busy time for the police in Brooklyn, and the 911 operator placed a call from the Jewish Center as very low priority, so no help arrived.

In desperation, someone at the Jewish Center called the JDL offices for assistance. Three JDL members from the office were dispatched to Kingsway to provide whatever assistance was needed. The JDL boys tried to protect the Jewish girls as they attempted to leave the premises, but they were outnumbered by the Italian kids, so they had difficulty helping the Jewish kids leave the premises safely. After several attempts to evacuate the premises peacefully failed, a fight broke out between the two factions. Outnumbered and facing a group of kids who were just as tough as they were, the situation deteriorated rapidly. Police assistance was needed if the Jewish kids were going to be able to extricate themselves from this dangerous situation.

Experience had taught the JDL members that in such a situation, when police were needed, they should call 911 and say the magic words: "Policeman down." Within minutes of the phone call to 911, several police cars arrived at the scene. Realizing that there was no "policeman down," the cops quickly separated the two sides and proceeded to arrest both the Italian kids and the JDL members, bringing them to the Avenue U police station. One of the JDL members had my number and called me around midnight to ask if I could come to the station and arrange for the release of the JDL kids or represent them at their arraignment in Night Court.

Since I lived just a few blocks from the police station, I quickly got dressed and sped to the police station, despite the late hour. Upon my arrival, I went to the desk sergeant and introduced myself as the lawyer for the Jewish kids. The police brought me up to date on what had transpired and then told me they had a problem resolving the situation. The sergeant indicated that the two groups were in the lock up, each group in a separate cell, where they were beginning to feel remorse over their actions as they each realized they would be facing the criminal justice system and spending the weekend in jail. For their part, the police did not want to formally arrest anyone, as an arrest would require a great deal of paperwork followed by bringing all of the defendants to court, probably meaning that the police involved would have to work on Sunday instead of having the day off from work. The sergeant invited me into an office, where I sat down with the arresting officers to see if we could come up with a solution to make this matter "go away."

When I suggested letting all the boys go home with a warning, the sergeant told me that the two groups were "jawing" at each other from their respective cells. Hence, the police were concerned that if they let the groups out, the fighting would recommence once they left the police station. My next suggestion was that they release the groups 30 minutes apart, thereby permitting one group to clear the area before the other group was released. This was quickly dismissed, as the police said that when they had taken everyone's name, the Jewish kids heard the addresses of the Italian kids, and the Italians knew where the Jewish kids lived. The police acknowledged that they had "screwed up" the identification process, and all they wanted to do was make sure that no further violence would follow.

It was then that I recalled the pact between Joe Colombo and Rabbi Meir Kahane, when Colombo became a supporter of the rabbi. Several police officers escorted me to the cell where the Italian boys were held. The sergeant suggested to the boys that they listen carefully to what I was going to tell them. I told the boys that while the police did not want to arrest anyone, they were hesitant to let everyone go lest the fight between the two factions resume once they were released from the confines of the police station. I also told them that the police were also very concerned about their safety because the Jewish kids were members of the JDL and were under the protection of the Colombo family, and the JDL boys were planning on calling their contact with the Colombo family as soon as they were released. I said that I had convinced them not to do so provided the other side was willing to let this matter end. I suggested that they accept this offer of the JDL members, because, otherwise, they could be in very serious trouble. Fortunately, they listened to me and agreed to the plan whereby the JDL members would be released first and the Italian boys about 30 minutes later.

By the time the police thanked me for my efforts, which meant that they would not have to go to court on Sunday, it was nearly 3:00 a.m., and I was very glad that I only lived ten minutes away. I arrived home wondering how many more JDL members would hear the story of the evening's events and begin to think I was the man to call if they needed a lawyer.

- 13 -

I AM A TAX MAN

MY INVOLVEMENT WITH THE JDL continued to grow due to my legal representation of JDL members and the continued isolation of the JDL by many in the organized Jewish community (which made it more difficult for us to find additional legal assistance).

One day, I received a call from a member of JDL's board of directors advising me that Rabbi Kahane was going to be his guest for Shabbat. Since I lived within walking distance of his home, he asked me if I wanted to join them for lunch on Shabbat. I readily agreed, as I was quite anxious to meet the Rabbi personally. At Shabbat lunch, I was introduced to the Rabbi as one of the few lawyers in the New York area who was willing to devote their time to defending JDL members. Upon hearing that I was a lawyer, the Rabbi immediately told me that he was negotiating a book deal with his publisher and he needed a lawyer to complete the negotiations.

As anxious as I was to be of assistance, I regrettably had to tell him that I was really a tax lawyer and did not think I could adequately represent him in the negotiations. Little did I know that "tax" was the magic word of the day. The Rabbi then asked me if I was familiar with tax-exempt organizations. I was pleased to tell him that I spent about 25% of my time working with organizations that were exempt from federal income tax under section 501(c)(3) of the Internal Revenue

Code. As soon as I told him that, he told me to forget about the book negotiations. Rather, he wanted to talk to me about obtaining tax-exempt status for what he called "the educational arm of the JDL."

The next day, he came to my home on Avenue R in Brooklyn to discuss a very pressing issue with me. He was struggling to raise large sums of money for all of the JDL's activities that he was anxious to implement. Even many of his most ardent supporters told him, "If I could deduct the money I give to the JDL from my taxes, I would substantially increase my contributions." The JDL's previous attempts to become a 501(c)(3) organization had been rejected by the Internal Revenue Service for obvious reasons. In the absence of the ability to provide tax deductions for contributors, the Rabbi did not see how he could raise money for the school he envisioned establishing.

I explained that I could not see the Internal Revenue Service ever granting the JDL or any organization affiliated with it 501(c)(3) status. Instead, I proposed that we set up a separate entity to operate the school/yeshivah that the Rabbi desperately wanted to open. If we did not taint the new entity with the JDL in any way, then I believed that I could apply for exemption with the hope of obtaining approval. My first recommendation was that we establish a new entity that did not include the words "defense" or even "league" in the title. My second recommendation was that none of the board of directors of the new entity be members of the board of the JDL. Finally, I informed the Rabbi that the organizations must maintain separate bank accounts and that there must be no co-mingling of funds. They would have to keep separate books and records. I would be responsible for compliance with the terms of the IRS determination letter (if we received one), so my address should be used as the legal mailing address of the organization.

Within three months of our meeting at my home, I had a letter from the Internal Revenue Service granting public charity status to the Jewish Identity Center of Jerusalem, Inc. If I was becoming somewhat of a hero with the JDL kids, Rabbi Kahane thought I was a miracle worker, as he was able to raise substantially more money than he ever had before. By the next summer, anyone driving along Route 52 between Ellenville and Liberty, New York in the Catskills, could see scores of teenagers in their *yarmulkes* and judo suits, engaging in vigorous self-defense maneuvers on the grounds of the Jewish Identity Center campus. As I listened to fellow summer residents of the Catskills complain about the scene of Jewish "ninjas" undergoing defense training in the open, I would say under my breath, "If only they knew who was responsible for getting the facility built..."

As a result of my obtaining a tax exemption, I could do no wrong in the eyes of Rabbi Kahane. After the Rabbi moved to Israel, there were several power struggles between different members of the JDL board regarding who would be Rabbi Kahane's successor. These disputes festered until the Rabbi returned to America and organized a convention wherein the members voted on who should be his successor. Unfortunately, the two factions could never really agree on who would control and count the ballots, and the Rabbi would not take sides lest it appear that he was not impartial in the election. On at least three occasions, he recommended that I be entrusted with the ballots, count them, and report the results back to the convention. This recommendation was always accepted by the different factions, which was a sign that I was accepted as an honest broker by all parties. I mention this fact because my reputation within the organization was a major factor that led to my difficulties with the FBI. However, before we get there, there are many more details in my story that have yet to be told.

- 14 -

NO VISA FOR YOU

A S THE ISSUE OF FREEDOM for Soviet Jewry continued to grow in importance for mainstream Jewish organizations, more and more people and organizations, especially rabbis from all denominations, were stepping forward to travel to Russia. In so doing, they were risking their personal freedom in order to smuggle religious articles into Russia for use by Soviet Jews. Trips to Russia by laypeople and rabbinic leaders was becoming a sign of their devotion to the cause of Soviet Jewry.

One Shabbat afternoon during this time, between the afternoon and evening prayer services, I was approached by a friend of mine who had a proposition for me. He had heard through the grapevine that I was very active in defending JDL members; therefore, he wanted to know if he could submit my name to the Student Struggle for Soviet Jewry (SSSJ) as someone who would be willing to travel to the Soviet Union and — illegally — bring *matzos* (the bread that is eaten over Passover) and Haggadahs (a book of various verses and prayers read at the Passover *Seder*) to the Russian Jews before Passover. These trips were risky, because a person taking such a trip was violating the laws of the communist regime and the Russian's use of their authority to arrest or detain someone was unpredictable.

As any orthodox Jew who works in federal taxes will tell you, as soon as they arrive, we immediately review the Gregorian calendar to see which Jewish holidays coincide with which dates on the Gregorian calendar. The key date is the day of the week of Rosh Hashanah. If it falls on a weekday, then vacation days will be used up for the holidays. One year, having put in many hours at work, I just needed a rest during the summer, but all of my vacation days had been used up by the time the holiday of Shavuot came around. Fortunately, the partner-in-charge of my group was very understanding and somehow arranged an extra week of vacation for me.

More important in the tax world, however, is when Passover occurs in relation to the week of April 15th. If Passover falls after April 15th, then the Jewish tax man need not concern himself with a tax season conflict. However, during the busiest week of the year, I often lost four days of work, which caused me a great deal of difficulty. One year, I worked through the night, leaving the office at 6 a.m., going directly to services for *siyum bechorim* (a special service on the morning preceding the Seder) and then returned to my office by 9 a.m. Because I needed to take time off work during the busiest time of the year, I had been working extremely long hours to make sure I got all of my work done by the time Passover arrived.

Personnel was concerned about the hours I was working, and they called me in for a meeting and suggested that I slow down a little bit. When I arrived at the office on Passover eve, I met the personnel director in the elevator, and he asked me what time I had gone home the previous night. When I told him "six o'clock," he said he was glad I had taken his advice and gone home early. I did not want to tell him it was six o'clock *in the morning*, but when I submitted my time report showing the 21 hours I had worked that day, he was a bit confused.

With this background, it is easy to understand why I knew the calendar by heart, so when I was asked if I could go to Russia and smuggle in *matzos*, I knew that Passover was after April 15th; thus, I would have the necessary days free to take the trip in March without jeopardizing my job. I anxiously awaited further details from my friend, as I thought a Russian trip would be an appropriate act for me given the time I had spent defending JDL members who were working so hard on behalf of Soviet Jewry.

Finally, he called me a few weeks before Passover.

"Who are you?" he asked.

"What do you mean 'who am I'?" I responded. "We have been friends for many years, what do you mean 'who am I'?"

"Well, we submit the names of our volunteers to the Soviet authorities for the issuance of visas. When they saw your name on the list, the Soviet official shouted, "Arthur Miller?! We will *never* give him a visa."

I knew then that everything I was doing to help the JDL in their actions for Soviet Jewry was worth it. Whether you agreed with their tactics or not, there was no arguing against the conclusion that the JDL was responsible for putting the issue of Soviet Jewry on the radar of so-called mainstream organizations. Even today, more than 50 years later, when my friends in Beit Shemesh ask me to join them on a tour of Russia, I refuse to go. I have no idea what inventory of names is maintained by the Russian authorities, but I refuse to take any chances and place myself within their jurisdiction. Call me paranoid if you will, but I am not taking chances with my freedom.

Interestingly, two years ago, in my role of film director for the Anglo over-55 group in Beit Shemesh, a group with over 175 members, I selected the film "Operation Wedding" for our annual fundraiser. The filmmaker is Anat Zalmanson-Kuznetsov, daughter of Sylva Zalmanson and Edward Kuznetsov, two Prisoners of Zion whose story of leaving Russia and emigrating to Israel is beautifully told in Anat's film. For me, it was unbelievable that I was talking to Sylva Zalmanson's daughter on a regular basis. I told Anat that her mother was a heroine and that I had worn a "Free Sylva Zalmanson" button for years.

When Anat attended the film and spoke after the presentation, someone from the audience asked a question about what her mother thought of the JDL and Rabbi Kahane. Much to my surprise, Anat was somewhat ambivalent about Rabbi Kahane and the JDL making her mother a household name back in the 1970s. Before Anat could explain her reasoning, I interrupted her and said, "I was one of Rabbi Kahane's lawyers, and this is not the time or place for that discussion." I also said it was not the forum for any debate, as we had all gathered just to view this incredible film. At a reception held after the film, several members of the audience who were supporters of Rabbi Kahane told me they were ready to do battle with Anat. I was glad I prevented any tension between my audience and Anat, as I did not want to detract from the film.

- 15 -

THE HUROK AFFAIR

O N JANUARY 26, 1972, A firebomb was detonated at the offices of Sol Hurok, the Jewish impresario who was responsible for bringing most of the Russian cultural artists to perform in the United States. This firebomb was different than any other act against the Soviets that the authorities had attributed to the JDL. The resulting fire and smoke resulted in the death of Iris Kones, a 27-year-old Jewish woman who was employed by the Hurok organization. An anonymous caller to various news agencies said the fires had been set to protest "the deaths and imprisonment of Soviet Jews." They shouted the slogan of the JDL: "Never again!" Although the JDL denied any involvement in the bombing, the police blamed the JDL and went after its members with a vengeance. Planting a smoke bomb in the men's room of Carnegie Hall to disrupt a performance was one thing, but this bombing, as Chief of Detectives Albert Seedman announced, "was murder."

To further make matters worse, the police had an informer inside the JDL who just happened to be the man responsible for making the bomb. Just about everyone involved in any JDL demonstration could anticipate being called in for questioning by the United States Attorney's Office, the New York Office of the FBI, or the Police Department of the City of New York. Despite the information provided by the informant, the prosecutors were quite anxious to get corroborating evidence as to who was involved in the Hurok bombing. In the absence of corroborating evidence, the informant's testimony can be torn apart upon cross-examination at trial as the defense attorney attempts to challenge his veracity by insisting that he received easy treatment in exchange for his testimony.

I was contacted by numerous young JDL members who had been called to appear before the US Attorney and the FBI to testify against the individuals whose identities had supposedly been disclosed by the informant. It seemed like almost every day that I was accompanying a young JDL member to the FBI office for questioning to meet with Special Agent Vincent M (last name withheld by me), who was in charge of the investigation. He questioned the young men and women about their whereabouts on that fatal day. When they responded that they were not present at the Hurok offices and that they did not have any knowledge of who was involved, the Special Agent insisted that someone else had told him that they had been involved in the bombing and suggested that if "they would come clean" and tell who else was involved, he could arrange a deal for them. The JDL members were wise to these tricks, and they kept insisting they were nowhere near Hurok's offices and that they had nothing to contribute to the FBI investigation.

After a few weeks of questioning the JDL members, Special Agent Vincent started to call me directly and tell me who I should bring in for questioning. This resulted in a funny moment when my wife and I were out for dinner for our birthdays, which are one day apart. My in-laws were babysitting our children, and it never dawned on me to tell my father-in-law that there was a possibility the FBI would call. Vincent called that evening, and my father-in-law, who never thought he would ever talk to a real FBI agent, answered the phone and almost went into shock when Vincent told him he was from the FBI and that I must call him back whenever I got home. When I walked in the door, my father-in-law, who was still shaken by the innocent encounter, told me that the FBI had called. He then informed me that he stood at attention while he was talking and called the agent "Sir," and he wanted to know if that was the correct thing to do. Imagine his shock when I called Vincent and my father-in-law realized I was on a first-name basis with the FBI agent. My father-in-law couldn't believe it when I told Vincent that I was too tired to talk to him and that he should never call me so late again.

My wife, Ronnie, once told me that Vincent had called during the daytime, and when she told him that I was at my office, he wanted to know my office number. Unsure as to whether I wanted my number given out, Ronnie said to him, "You are the FBI. I am sure you can find the number by yourself."

- 16 -

I AM THREATENED
WITH ARREST

I N ADDITION TO BEING QUESTIONED by the FBI, JDL members were also being questioned by the United States Attorneys' office, who was hoping to obtain evidence about who was involved in the Hurok bombing.

One evening, I received a call at home from a teenage girl I did not know, and she said she had received a phone call from Mr. Henry Putzel, an Assistant United States Attorney who had requested her presence at his office on Foley Square on Friday at 2 p.m. The young girl wanted to know if I was available to go with her to meet with Mr. Putzel. I agreed to go with her on Friday afternoon and suggested we meet on Thursday evening so that I could learn if she'd had any involvement in the Hurok matter and to prepare her for the good cop/bad cop routine of the Assistant United States Attorneys who would be present at the questioning. We met at the JDL office in mid-Manhattan and proceeded to a stairwell, where the threat of a listening device was less likely.

I started to explain that one of the government attorneys, usually Mr. Putzel, would play the role of the "bad cop" and try to frighten her into making a damning admission. The other United States Attorney, probably Mr. Joseph Jaffe, would try and calm Putzel down and give the impression that he was on the side of the witness. As I tried to prepare her for what to expect, she quickly interrupted me and told me that she had an uncle who smuggled arms into Israel for the Irgun before Israel's independence in 1948, thereby violating the United States embargo on arms shipments to Israel. In so doing, he risked arrest by the British if he was caught illegally entering the country. "Now that you know my background, do you think I am afraid of the FBI?" she asked. I was duly impressed and told her I would meet her the next day at 1:30 p.m. on the steps of the main entrance to the Foley Square courthouse. As Shabbat started around 4:30 p.m. and I had about a 30-minute subway ride from the courthouse to my home in Flatbush, I stressed the importance of being there on time.

That Friday was a cold wintery day, and when I alighted from the subway station, I was not pleased to discover that an icy rain had begun to fall. *Why,* I thought to myself, *did I tell her to meet me outside and not in the lobby where I could keep warm?!* Not wanting to take the chance of missing her, I waited outside for her to arrive, all the while shivering in the cold and constantly wiping the icy rain off of my eyeglasses. By 1:45 p.m., with no one showing up at the main entrance who looked like a nice young Jewish girl, I had no choice but to go inside and hopefully warm up. By 2:15 p.m., I thought perhaps she had been foolish enough to go up to Mr. Putzel's office by herself, so I went upstairs to his office. Before we even had a chance to exchange pleasantries, Mr. Putzel told me that his office was preparing a warrant for my arrest.

To say I was shocked is an understatement. I told him that the first thing he should do is offer me a hot cup of tea because I was freezing. After I'd had my cup of tea, I would be happy to find out what he was talking about. Putzel informed me that my client was not waiting for me in his office. Rather, after she spoke to me on Thursday evening, she hopped on an El Al plane to Israel. "You must have known she was not going to appear today, and your meeting with her was just a ruse to throw us off track. We are considering pressing charges against you for conspiring to obstruct justice."

"You must be mad, Henry," I replied. "If I had known she was not going to show up, I would not have been waiting outside in the freezing rain. Besides, if you knew what she told me, then it appears that someone's telephone has been the subject of a wiretap, and if that is what threw you off track, then you deserve it. Just because you were duped by a teenager doesn't mean you should threaten me with arrest."

I stormed out of his office impressed by my client's nerve. Not being under subpoena to appear before the United States Attorney, she left the country and would be able to return when things calmed down. I never saw or heard from her again, and I have no idea if she returned to America or stayed in Israel. Unfortunately, though, I was not through with Henry Putzel.

- 17 -

SHHH! HE THINKS I'M
TEACHING HIM ENGLISH

THERE IS AN OLD JOKE that I think is attributable to Myron Cohen, the masterful Jewish storyteller, about a waiter who had been working at Schmulka Bernstein's Restaurant on Essex Street on New York's Lower East Side. Bernstein's was famous for developing kosher Chinese food. As anyone who visited the restaurant knew, half the waiters were American, and, to add a little bit of authenticity, the other half were Chinese. According to the joke, a patron was ordering his dinner and being waited upon by an American waiter who then gave instructions, in Yiddish, to a Chinese waiter. The Chinese waiter answered the American waiter in perfect Yiddish.

"That's remarkable," replied the patron. "I never heard a Chinese person speak such perfect Yiddish."

"Shh," said the American waiter. "He thinks I'm teaching him English."

I have never been able to verify the authenticity of this story, but I have it on good authority that it is true. At least once a week, after a JDL board of directors meeting, the group would adjourn and go to Schmulka Bernstein's for dinner. Supposedly, one of the Chinese waiters was an undercover agent for the FBI and was always assigned to wait on the JDL group. The waiter stayed in close enough proximity to the JDL table to hear the discussion, which he would then report back to his superiors. For their part, the diners ignored the waiter's presence near their table, as they only heard him speak in very broken English; therefore, they assumed that he could not understand their conversations.

- 18 -

THE INFORMANT

IN JUNE 1972, FOUR MEMBERS of the JDL were arrested in connection with the firebombing at the Hurok offices and at the offices of Columbia Artists Management, another agency that was heavily involved in bringing Soviet talent to the United States.

Three of the four men, Sheldon Davis (age nineteen), Stuart Cohen (age nineteen), and Sheldon Siegel (age twenty-five), were linked to the bombings of both the Hurok offices and the Columbia Artists Management building (in the latter case, no one was injured). These three were held in lieu of bail of $35,000 each on federal charges of setting off an explosive device in offices "used in activities affecting interstate and foreign commerce." Because of the death of Iris Kones in the Hurok offices, there was a possibility that the charges against the three men would lead to the death penalty. The fourth arrested individual was Jeffrey Smilow, a seventeen-year-old yeshivah senior. He was charged in the Columbia bombing only. Smilow was arraigned in Manhattan Criminal Court on second-degree arson charges, carrying a maximum penalty of 25 years. He was later released on $3,500 bail.

As I had nothing to do with any of the Hurok defendants, I assumed that the arrests were made as the result of good police investigations, including, perhaps, interrogations of one or more of the JDL members I accompanied to the grand jury. In February 1973, as the scheduled date for the Hurok trial approached, the federal government asked the judge to sever the trial of Sheldon Siegel from that of Sheldon Davis and Stuart Cohen. The reasons given for this request were that Sheldon Siegel was a government informant who had provided information leading to the indictments, that he had testified before the grand jury, and that he would be called as a witness at trial under a grant of immunity.

The circumstances under which Siegel became a government informant involved a gross violation of the rules applicable to wire-tapping and other actions used by law enforcement officials in their investigation of criminal activities. In 1970, then Attorney General John Mitchell ordered the FBI to install a wiretap in the JDL offices in Manhattan. As anyone who has watched any of the numerous crime programs on television knows, a judge's permission must be obtained in order to install the wiretap. However, for whatever reason, no such judicial approval was obtained for the wiretapping of the JDL offices. Thus, the surveillance, which lasted in excess of a year, was conducted without judicial sanction. The government admitted that the unauthorized wiretaps were illegal. As a further breach of the rules, the government did not maintain the tapes of the wiretaps, and government representatives admitted that the tapes had been destroyed erroneously. Logs of the conversations were presented in lieu of the actual copies of the tapes.

On April 22, 1971, while the FBI's JDL tap was in operation, a bomb exploded at the offices of the Amtorg Trading Corporation, the home of the Russian Trade Mission in New York. A New York City Police Department investigation of this bombing ultimately led to physical surveillance of Sheldon Siegel and, eventually, to his arrest in a parking garage on June 4, 1971. At that time of his arrest in the garage, Siegel's car was searched illegally. The illegal search disclosed fragments of wire, several pieces of plastic, a can of mace, a small film capsule filled with gunpowder, a cardboard tube with an attached fuse, and ten empty alarm clock boxes. Siegel's automobile was impounded, and on June 29, 1971, he was indicted on state charges for possession of explosives.

Following the seizure of his car, Siegel met with various members of the criminal justice system in an unsuccessful attempt to obtain the return of his car. During these efforts, he came in contact with a number of law enforcement officials, including Assistant District Attorneys, an Assistant United States Attorney for the Eastern District of New York, an officer from the Alcohol and Firearm Division of the United States Treasury Department, and Detectives Santo Parola and Joseph Gibney of the New York City Police Department. These law enforcement personnel attempted to coax Siegel into cooperating with their investigation of the JDL's activities, particularly with reference to the bombing of the offices of the Amtorg Trading Corporation on April 22, 1971.

All of the negotiations between Siegel and Detective Parola, who became Siegel's primary contact within law enforcement, were held without the presence of Siegel's attorney. Parola advised Siegel that the materials they had found in his car had led the police to conclude that Siegel had been involved in the Amtorg bombing. During the summer of 1971, Siegel, who still had not consulted with his attorney, agreed to cooperate with the police in their investigation of the JDL. Shortly thereafter, on September 8, 1971, he was indicted by a federal grand jury in the Eastern District of New York for the Amtorg bombing. By indicting him, law enforcement officials believed that they had successfully protected his cover as an informant. From the United States Attorney and Detective Parola, Siegel received a note advising him that he would not be prosecuted in the Amtorg case.

Siegel advised Parola that he wished to discuss his immunity with his attorney. The authorities advised against it. Parola admitted that he repeatedly advised Siegel not to discuss the question with his attorney or to get an attorney who was not affiliated with the JDL. Thereafter, Siegel continued to speak frequently with Parola and Gibney, and he continued to provide information concerning planned JDL activities against Soviet officials and offices. On December 15, 1971, however, without Siegel's knowledge, the government initiated a warrantless electronic surveillance on his home telephone, and the FBI overheard many of his conversations. The surveillance, the illegality of which the government conceded, was maintained through March 1, 1972. The dates, of course, are highly significant, at least in Siegel's eyes, because the recorded time period included the date of the Hurok bombing on January 26, 1972. The tapes of these interceptions were destroyed by the government. After the Hurok incident, Parola attempted to elicit information from Siegel regarding JDL involvement in the affair. It was not until May 7, 1972, however, that Siegel disclosed to Parola the names of the participants in the Hurok and Columbia bombings, including his own.

In summary, the government's knowledge of JDL's alleged involvement in the Hurok bombing was obtained from Sheldon Siegel, himself a participant (and principle bombmaker) in the bombing. More importantly, Siegel's cooperation was obtained illegally, including through warrantless wiretaps and a denial of his right to consult with his attorney. This misconduct by the police eventually led to a dismissal of all charges against all three Hurok defendants. However, in May 1973, the government was preparing for the trial, and when my phone rang, I very reluctantly became a participant.

- 19 -

THE HUROK TRIAL

SOMETIME IN LATE MAY, I received a call from Bert Zweibon, an attorney and one of the senior JDL executives, asking me to come to his office to discuss my participation in the trial. At first, I thought it must be a joke. While I had gained much experience during the time of my involvement in JDL matters, all of the experience was, what I would consider, minor. Zweibon was now asking me to get involved in a highly publicized, potentially capital case, which was clearly beyond my comfort level. Zweibon tried to reassure me that I would receive guidance from one of New York's most capable criminal attorneys: Barry Slotnick. As Joe Colombo's lawyer, Barry had introduced Joe Colombo and Rabbi Kahane. Once again, I tried to dissuade Zweibon from getting me involved, but, just like Bob Persky did when he first called me to help out, Zweibon pleaded with me that there was no one else.

The government had three witnesses whom they intended to call at trial: Sheldon Siegel, the informant whose trial was severed from the other defendants, Richard Huss, and Jeffrey Smilow. Smilow and Huss were two teenagers whose involvement in the Hurok case was peripheral at best. The jury was impaneled, and Sheldon Siegel was the first witness called to the stand after opening statement. After he was sworn in, Siegel refused to answer any questions. By this time, Siegel, who had been denied counsel consistently and who became an informant due to numerous violations of his constitutional rights, including the illegality of the various wiretaps, was no longer without counsel. Due to all of the government misconduct in his case, Siegel was now represented by Professor Alan Dershowitz of Harvard Law School and his team.

Usually, a witness refusing to testify in a criminal trial invokes the Fifth Amendment of the Bill of Rights, which protects a witness from incriminating himself. Siegel did not raise any Fifth Amendment privilege issues, as the government was prepared to offer him immunity from prosecution in exchange for his testimony. Siegel's refusal to testify was based on the numerous violations of his constitutional rights, in the absence of which the government would never have learned of his identity and involvement in the Amtorg bombing and would not have had anything with which to threaten Siegel in order to compel his cooperation.

When a witness, under a grant of immunity, refuses to testify, the judge can find the witness to be in contempt of court and arrest him on the spot for his refusal. Generally, the recalcitrant witness will be imprisoned until he testifies or when the trial is over. In Siegel's case, the trial judge, Judge Bauman, believed that the constitutional issues with respect to Siegel were so compelling that, while he did find Siegel to be in contempt of court, he nevertheless released him on bail. Professor Dershowitz indicated his intent to appeal the contempt citation based on the violation of Siegel's rights, thereby preventing him from being compelled to testify.

With Siegel's testimony on hold pending resolution of his appeal, which by law would be heard on an expedited basis since a jury had already been empaneled, the next two witnesses scheduled to be called were Richard Huss and Jeffery Smilow. Prior to the date of their testimony, I met with Barry Slotnick, who told me that I should introduce myself to the court as Richard Huss' attorney when he was called to the stand and before he was sworn in. I should then ask the prosecuting attorney to confirm that I had not been the victim of an illegal wiretap by the United States Attorney's Office, the CIA, the FBI, or any other law enforcement agency. Robert P. Leighton, the attorney for Jeffrey Smilow, made the same request on his behalf. Henry Putzel, the same Assistant United States Attorney who had wanted to arrest me when a client of mine ran off to Israel, responded that he could not confirm that we had not been subject to the aforementioned wiretaps. Judge Bauman then gave Mr. Putzel seven days to respond to my request and adjourned the trial for a week. One week later, we were back in court, and Henry Putzel confirmed to the court that neither me nor Robert Leighton had been illegally wiretapped by the various government agencies.

Judge Bauman was now satisfied that the trial could continue, and Richard Huss was recalled to the stand. Mr. Huss, a seventeen-year-old from Staten Island, refused to answer any questions concerning the Hurok incident. Judge Bauman wanted to know why Huss was refusing to answer any questions, since the government had granted him immunity from prosecution, thereby depriving Huss of the defense of the Fifth Amendment. Huss explained that he had been advised by his rabbi that it was not permitted for a Jew to testify against another Jew in a non-Jewish court.

Bauman then explained in clear and precise language that the teachings of Huss' rabbi were not acceptable in a United States Court and that if Huss did not respond to the questions put to him, the judge would find him in contempt of the court, subjecting him to immediate arrest. Judge Bauman explained that the key to the jail cell was in Mr. Huss' control. "You can open the door to your cell by letting the court know when you are ready to answer the questions put to you. If you continue to refuse to answer any questions, you will stay in jail until this trial is over."

The judge then asked me if I had discussed these matters with my client and whether my client fully understood what was going to happen to him. I assured Judge Bauman that I had explained all of the consequences of his refusal to testify, and Mr. Huss fully understood the consequences of this refusal. The judge then ordered the bailiff to place Mr. Huss under arrest until he chose to open the door to his cell. My motion to release Mr. Huss on bail was denied. I announced my intention to appeal Mr. Huss's arrest, and the judge told me that the expedited appeal rules applicable to Mr. Siegel would similarly be applied to Mr. Huss. With that, Richard Huss was taken to the Federal Detention Center on West Street until the end of the trial.

After Huss's arrest, Jeffrey Smilow was called to the stand. The same scenario that had just played out with Huss then transpired between the court, Smilow, and Robert Leighton. When Smilow was removed from the court and taken to the Federal Detention Center, Henry Putzel announced to the court that he had no further witnesses.

All three witnesses that the government intended to call to the stand had refused to testify, and the government's case now depended on the outcome of the expedited Court of Appeals process regarding the contempt of court proceedings against the three young men. Reluctantly, Judge Bauman had to call yet another recess in the trial pending the results of the appeals process. Three weeks had passed since the jury had been selected, opening statements had been made, and still not one piece of evidence had been presented to the court.

The newspapers were very critical of the government's lawyers, and as I left the courtroom, I got the impression that Henry Putzel was furious at members of the defense team, including me, for being, in his eyes, the group that was responsible for the bad publicity being directed at him. The day after this latest recess, the court proceedings were reported in detail on the front page of the New York Law Journal, a publication designed for and utilized by lawyers to apprise them of what was happening in the law.

Until this time, while the regular press had been reporting on the trial, my name had not appeared in the newspapers. I had been referred to by the various newspapers as "Mr. Huss' attorney." I was quite pleased that my name had not been in the papers for several reasons. First of all, it was important that my office not know what I was involved in, and I did not want them to find out. Secondly, I did not want my mother to know of my involvement, because she was "the worrying sort." One of my mother's neighbors on Grand Street was a local attorney, who, upon receipt of his copy of the New York Law Journal, went to my parents' apartment and told my mother, "Arthur is involved in some major case. He made the front page of the New York Law Journal." Of course, my office also found out, and, to put it mildly, they were very unhappy that I was spending so many hours involved in a major criminal case.

- 20 -

PREPARING FOR THE APPEAL

WITH THE ARRESTS OF JEFFREY Smilow and Richard Huss, I had about ten days before I would have to argue before Chief Judge Irving Kaufman and two other Court of Appeals judges that the refusal of Smilow and Huss to testify was constitutionally protected under the freedom of religion clause of the First Amendment. Sunday was going to be a long day at the law library as I began to plan my arguments.

In the meantime, on the second day of their incarceration, I received a call from Mrs. Smilow advising me that the prison authorities were not meeting the requirements of prisoners who observed the Jewish laws of kosher food. Mrs. Smilow said that her son, Jeffrey, and Richard Huss had been keeping a diet of a hardboiled egg and a slice of bread — for breakfast, lunch, and supper. The boys, who were not happy about being prisoners in the Federal Detention Center, were certainly less happy with the cuisine that they were being fed. This was 1973, and the court battle for the right of Jewish prisoners to obtain kosher food had not even begun.

The prison officials knew that both the Smilow and Huss appeals would be argued in an expedited procedure. Since their refusal to testify was based on a religious principle, it had been decided that I would argue the case before the Court of Appeals. I had been told by the court that I had ten minutes to make my arguments. Accordingly, the prison officials knew that I needed unlimited access to Huss and Smilow in preparation for their appeal. Thus, every day at 12 p.m. for the next two weeks, a member of the Smilow family met me at my office and drove me to the Federal Detention Center to meet with my clients.

Upon entering the prison, I was asked to show my legal identification and to declare whether I had any weapons in my briefcase. I notified the prison guards that I did not have any weapons but that I needed immediate access to both Huss and Smilow as I prepared for an expedited appeal. In my briefcase was a legal pad and meat sandwiches prepared for the boys by Mrs. Smilow. Admittance took several minutes, as I had to sign in and then wait until the heavy metal gates were opened and I was admitted to a meeting room. I waited in the room for Smilow and Huss, and when they were escorted in, dressed in their orange prison uniforms, I quickly opened my briefcase and took out the two sandwiches that I had brought for them. Both boys were quite hungry, so they gobbled down the sandwiches. Meanwhile, using my lunch hour to provide food for them, I could only look on and absorb the smells of the sandwiches. To this day, I am not sure why I didn't ask Mrs. Smilow to provide a sandwich for me. After they finished eating and Jeffrey Smilow, who was a religious yeshivah student, said grace, I reminded them that, as Judge Bauman had told them, they had the keys to unlock the cell door. This reminder was a mere formality on my part, as I knew neither of the boys had any intention of testifying at the trial, regardless of the consequences of their actions. I was then chauffeured back to my office, usually arriving at around 1:30 p.m., leaving me no time for my own lunch.

On Sunday, I went to the law library at Brooklyn Law School to research support for Smilow and Huss' refusal to testify. Somehow, I had to convince the Court of Appeals that compelling Huss and Smilow to testify was a violation of their First Amendment right to the freedom to practice their religion. By agreement, I would present the oral argument supporting our position, and any written submission would be taken care of by Robert Leighton. I had also been advised by Barry Slotnick that the ten-minute rule would be strictly enforced. Unless one of the three judges hearing our appeal wanted further clarification, I would be stopped mid-sentence as soon as the ten minutes was up.

The United States Constitution is a remarkable document. The First Amendment provides that Congress must not make any law respecting the establishment of a religion or prohibiting the free exercise thereof. It was the last phrase, "prohibiting the free exercise thereof" that was my only real basis for challenging the civil contempt citation imposed by Judge Bauman on Richard Huss and Jeffrey Smilow. In the Jewish Amidah prayer that is recited three times a day, we say, "Let there be no hope for informers," a prayer that has been interpreted by many to mean that a Jew should not testify against a fellow Jew in a non-Jewish court. Accordingly, compelling Huss or Smilow to inform against Davis and Cohen would mean that the government was interfering in Huss and Smilow's free exercise of their religion.

In addition, Jewish law commands each person to "make for himself a rabbi" to whom he is obligated to listen. Both Huss and Smilow said that their rabbi was Rabbi Meir Kahane, to whom they were obligated to listen on matters of Jewish law. Rabbi Kahane had advised them that they were not permitted to testify against another Jew in a non-Jewish court. A conflicting Jewish law provides that we are supposed to observe the laws of our country of residence. Furthermore, the government has an interest to maintain law and order, thereby placing a restriction on the free exercise of religion as stated in the First Amendment. The right of the state to maintain law and order appears to conflict with a person's constitutional protection to practice his religion as he desires.

In my research, I found a few cases that provided that the rights of the individual prevail over the interests of the state when a "cardinal principle" of one's religion is involved. The question that I had to address was: What is a cardinal principle of the Jewish religion? Is the prohibition against testifying in a secular court a cardinal principle? I knew Judaism's value of human life meant that one was permitted to violate most of the 613 commandments of the Torah to save a life, but there are three exceptions to this rule: idolatry, murder, and engaging in incestuous relations. Somehow, I had ten minutes to convince the three judges on the Court of Appeals that refusing to testify against a fellow Jew in a secular court was almost at the level of the three big exceptions to saving a life.

- 21 -

A STRANGE PHONE CALL

A FEW DAYS BEFORE THE APPEAL date, I received a telephone call from an individual who identified himself as Richard Huss' uncle. He wanted to know what my plans were for the forthcoming appeal. I tried to explain everything to him as I would if I were talking to a layman. Thus, my explanation was very basic. However, he interrupted me and told me that he was a professor of constitutional law and that I could skip the basics and get into my planned arguments.

"You are a constitutional law professor?" I exclaimed in disbelief. "Then why aren't you arguing the appeal on behalf of your nephew?"

He told me that he had offered to represent Richard in the appeal, but he had been refused. Richard would only accept me, a JDL lawyer, as his attorney. I was incredulous. I said it made no sense to have me argue the appeal when his uncle was infinitely more qualified than I was. I offered to reason with Richard when I next brought the two boys their lunch at the prison. He did not think it would work, as Richard was adamant that his uncle should not represent him in his appeal. I then offered to resign as his attorney so that his uncle could step into my place. I was advised that my resignation could be viewed by the court as a further delaying tactic and I could be held in contempt of court for the delaying tactics. Remember, the jury had been seated for several weeks without any testimony being heard, and neither the judge nor the government was pleased with this delay. Finally, it was decided that without Richard's consent, I had no option but to continue with his appeal.

- 22 -

I MEET WITH A TZADDIK

WITH THE APPEALS DATE OF June 8th rapidly approaching, I began to get my thoughts together on how to convince the distinguished panel of judges at the Court of Appeals that Huss and Smilow should not be forced to testify because doing so interfered with the free practice of their religion. I must admit that even I was not convinced that my arguments would carry the day.

Sensing my insecurity, a colleague tried to reassure me by reminding me that the Chief Judge of the Court was a Jew. Therefore, he would have sympathy for these two nice Jewish teenagers. I had to remind my colleague that this Honorable Judge Irving Kaufman was the same judge who, back in 1951, sentenced Julius and Ethel Rosenberg to the electric chair.

I knew that if I was going to give the boys any chance in their appeal, I needed the assistance of a Torah sage to help me prepare my arguments. Fortunately, since I grew up on the Lower East Side, the rabbi from my regular synagogue was the esteemed Torah scholar Rabbi Nisson L. Alpert *a"h*. Over the years that I attended the "Third Street Shul" for prayer services, my family had become very close with the Rabbi and his family. I called the Rabbi, told him my predicament, and asked him if he could take a few hours out of his busy schedule and fortify me with the basis of my arguments before the Court of Appeals. Rabbi Alpert was delighted to help and told me I should call him by 6 a.m. the following morning to see when we could discuss the matter further before he left for services at his alma mater, the Mesivta Tiferes Yerushalayim yeshivah on East Broadway, and then to Yeshiva University.

I was up bright and early and called him before 6 a.m. as I had been instructed. Unfortunately, his wife informed me that I had just missed him and that I should try him after 8 p.m. that night. The Rabbi did not return home until midnight, and when I called from my parents' home on the Lower East Side, I was very apologetic for calling so late. Knowing that he had left his house before 6 a.m., I felt terrible for disturbing him while he was eating his dinner after midnight, but Rabbi Alpert told me to come right over. I thought I was keeping him from his much-needed sleep, but he told me that he had been busy teaching Torah to his many students at Yeshiva University all day and this was his chance to learn Torah for himself. It would be several hours before he would actually go to sleep. I quickly realized that Rabbi Alpert functioned on just two or three hours of sleep a night, with the remaining 20 or 21 hours in his day devoted to teaching and learning Torah. I was truly in the presence of a tzaddik (holy person).

We spent over an hour together, as he provided me with authoritative sources supporting the importance of a Jewish person not testifying against a fellow Jew in a secular court as well as the importance of following the dictates of the Rabbi who explained the law to that person. As the hours turned into morning and I returned home to Brooklyn, I felt just a bit more confident in my ability to condense the law into a concise ten-minute presentation. Whether I would be able to convince Judge Kaufman and his fellow judges that these rules were "cardinal principles" of Jewish law was another matter.

- 23 -

THE APPEAL

CCORDING TO THE EXPEDITED PROCEDURES established for the appeal, the case was argued on June 12, 1973, a typical steamy June day in New York City. I was so wound up that my nerves twitched all night and I did not get a good night's sleep as I went over in my mind, time and time again, what I would say in my ten minutes before the judges of the Court of Appeals. I arrived at the courthouse with plenty of time to spare, clutching my briefcase within which I carried my notes and a small book entitled *Shulchan Aruch* (The Code of Jewish Law).

As I reviewed my proposed arguments with Robert Leighton, I was blown away when Professor Alan Dershowitz of Harvard Law School sauntered in followed by a team of lawyers, many of whom I recognized from the news. They were trailed by a bevy of Harvard Law students pushing a large book trolley, laden down with the numerous cases that Professor Dershowitz intended to present to the esteemed judges. I was struck with a severe case of inadequacy and asked the much more experienced Robert Leighton if he wanted to switch places with me. Bob gave me a quick and emphatic refusal, and in we went to the prestigious courtroom to face the three judges sitting majestically on high.

It seemed that I had something in common with the three judges: I was anxious to make my arguments so that I could listen to Professor

Dershowitz argue on behalf of Sheldon Siegel. True to the schedule, I was granted ten minutes to make my arguments, during which I recited my presentation and answered one question from Judge Kaufman. Then, I sat down to listen to Prof. Dershowitz make his case.

The Siegel appeal lasted for more than 50 minutes before Judge Kaufman stopped it and advised everyone that the court would take all three appeals under advisement and that we should expect an expedited decision. Robert Leighton and I made motions to release Huss and Smilow on bail while their appeal was under consideration. Our request for bail was denied in both cases, a strong indication that the judges' initial reaction to our clients was not favorable. Judge Kaufman then granted Prof. Dershowitz's request to continue bail for Sheldon Siegel.

Following the appeal, there was nothing to do but wait for the decision. Each day at noon, I drove down to the federal prison on West Street to deliver lunch to Smilow and Huss. I was not optimistic about winning our appeal, as I believed if the judges were leaning in our direction, Smilow and Huss would have been granted bail during the appeals process. True to their word, the decision was expedited. On June 26th, I received a call from the court advising me that the judges were prepared to announce their decision.

I raced to the courthouse to obtain a copy of the decision. About 95% of the lengthy decision dealt with the court's analysis of the Siegel decision. The judges agreed with Prof. Dershowitz that Siegel's rights had been grossly violated through the illegal wiretaps and denial of his right to counsel, and they dismissed the contempt charges against him. The contempt citations against Huss and Smilow were affirmed. The Court stated that while I had indeed shown distinctions between the facts of our case and similar cases requiring witnesses to testify, they were distinctions that did not make a difference in an American court. Accordingly, the order of civil contempt against Richard Huss and Jeffrey Smilow was affirmed.

As I read the decision, dejected by the adverse decision, the clerk said that I had in fact received an "atta boy" from Judge Kaufman. He further stated that the fact that the court recognized the distinctions I had raised was the equivalent of a pat on my back. Nevertheless, I could not help but feel the pain of my first defeat as both the Smilow and Huss contempt citations were upheld.

- 24 -

COURT RECONVENES

TWO DAYS LATER, COURT RECONVENED. After all that had taken place over the last month, the proceedings were almost anti-climactic. Assistant United States Attorney Henry Putzel had only three witnesses to call. The first witness was Sheldon Siegel, and he had refused to testify. As Siegel was successful in his appeal, he again refused to answer any questions. Since he could not be threatened with contempt of court, he was dismissed.

Attorney Putzel then called Richard Huss to the stand, and he continued to refuse to testify despite the admonition of Judge Bauman that he faced criminal contempt charges if he continued to refuse to testify. Jeffrey Smilow was then called to the stand, and, likewise, he refused to testify. Further attempting to give both young men the opportunity to reconsider their decision, Judge Bauman warned them that in a criminal contempt trial, they could be sentenced to life in prison. Despite this threat, both Huss and Smilow continued in their refusal to testify. With no other witnesses and with no testimony ever offered into the record, the judge had no choice but to dismiss the charges against Cohen and Davis. The judge told the jury, "It is my duty to tell you that the government is unable to proceed with the trial of the defendants in this case because three young associates of theirs have refused to testify in the case."

The trial was over for me. With the end of the trial, Huss and

Smilow were released from their confinement. Eventually, both were charged with criminal contempt and were sentenced to a year in a federal detention center in Kentucky. While in prison, Huss and Smilow unsuccessfully sued the federal government for the right to receive kosher food in jail. It was not until two years later, when Rabbi Kahane was the person seeking kosher food, that the right of Jewish prisoners to obtain kosher food was finally ordered by the court.

After my involvement, I never saw or heard from Richard Huss again. To the best of my knowledge, he went into the family's business on Staten Island. About a decade later, I met Jeffrey Smilow, who I believe went on to become an engineer, and asked him if he had any regrets. "I believed in what I was doing, and I have never had any regrets about my actions."

- 25 -

THE END OF AN ERA

WHEN I WAS GROWING UP on the Lower East Side, I usually went with my friends to the Young Israel Synagogue on East Broadway on Shabbat mornings. On Rosh Hashanah and Yom Kippur, my brother and I, along with the rest of the family living in the neighborhood, went to the Chevra Bechurim Synagogue on East Third Street. Originally, the Synagogue was on Lewis Street, and I found out that my maternal grandfather, Morris Schwartz, who died before I was born, was the long-standing President of the congregation.

As the Lower East Side went through a period of urban renewal, many of the old-time synagogues, like the one on Lewis Street, were taken by eminent domain, and the congregations received a respectable sum of money for their buildings. Several of these congregations that no longer had a large enough membership to build or renovate a new synagogue merged into one congregation, combining their proceeds to renovate a synagogue building on East Third Street between Avenue C and Avenue D. Thus, the old-time family synagogue on Lewis Street where my grandfather was President for many years became known as the Chevra Bechurim B'nai Menashe Ahavas Achim, the name signifying the five congregations that had merged into one and renovated an old synagogue into a truly beautiful one that was, to say the least, out of place on East Third Street.

By the time I was married in 1967, the Chevra had become our regular place for Shabbat prayer services and was no longer just a place where we went for the Jewish holidays. I am sure the switch to the Chevra occurred due to our affinity for Rabbi Nisson Alpert. Each week, we took the longer walk to East Third Street from Grand Street, oftentimes braving anti-Semitic remarks, barbs, and even projectiles as we traversed the no-longer Jewish neighborhood between Grand and East Third Street. In 1971, Ronnie and I moved to Avenue R in the Flatbush section of Brooklyn, and by 1973, my uncle, Sol Schwartz, the original Noah Zark Pizza man, was President of the Synagogue, a position held by his father a generation earlier.

With my historical ties to the Chevra, it was very difficult for me when I woke up one Friday morning in October 1973, turned on the news, and heard the report that a 75-year-old synagogue on the Lower East Side had been extensively damaged after a firebomb had been hurled into the building. When the news reporter gave the address as 297 East Third Street, between Avenues C and D, I knew it was my synagogue, and the rage burned through me probably as intense as the fire inside the structure. Fortunately, the building was empty at the time. Nevertheless, 13 firemen who had helped put out the fire were treated for smoke inhalation, which suggests the ferocity of the blaze.

Newspaper reports indicated that the fire had begun near the ark of the synagogue (where the precious Torah scrolls are kept) and spread quickly to the wooden pews, prayer books, and prayer shawls. All of the windows, many of them stained glass, were broken in the blaze. As a result of the mergers of the various congregations, the Chevra possessed a large collection of Torah scrolls, most of which were damaged by the smoke but were reparable. Rabbi Nisson Alpert attributed the cause of the fire to youth gangs in the neighborhood. "This is a systematic plan by some gangs in the neighborhood to drive out all remnants of the Jewish community on the Lower East

Side," he said. The Chevra decided to abandon the neighborhood and merged yet again — this time with a small synagogue on East Broadway. Following the fire and the death of my Uncle Sol shortly after the fire, my father became the President there and served in that capacity until he was killed in a car crash in Israel in 1995.

Due to my family's long-standing relationship with the synagogue, it was no surprise that I was in great distress the morning after the fire. Not knowing what to do but certainly seeking revenge, I called Russel Kelner of the JDL to see if he had any suggestions. We decided that when we heard that an arrest had been made, I would go the arraignment and see if I could learn the identity of the perpetrators. The plan was to teach them a lesson about what happens to those who destroy Jewish property and to ensure that this lesson resonated throughout the local community. An arrest was never made; thus, our plans for revenge never materialized. Nevertheless, it was good to know that there was an organization that would not hesitate to protect Jewish interests.

- 26 -

ARAFAT COMES TO TOWN

F OLLOWING THE HUROK TRIAL, MY court activities seemed
to decline, and my workload at my office kept me very busy.
During this period, I was doing quite a bit of speaking on
behalf of the JDL in and around the New York Metropolitan Area. I
was the speaker when Rabbi Kahane was not in the United States or
when David Fisch, who succeeded the Rabbi as the acting head of the
JDL after Rabbi Kahane moved to Israel, was not available. I enjoyed
these speaking engagements. Speaking in synagogues and temples
in all five boroughs, I realized that the rank-and-file membership
supported the JDL, even when the rabbi of the synagogue did not
attend my presentation as a means of showing his disagreement with
the JDL's tactics.

One memorable evening occurred in the winter of 1973, after
the imposition of the Arab oil boycott, when a request came from a
synagogue in Binghamton, New York, about 200 miles from my home
in Brooklyn. I advised the group that it was not possible to travel to
Binghamton under normal circumstances in the dead of winter — and
surely not during an oil shortage. Satisfied that I had been reasonable
in turning down the engagement, I was quite surprised when the
president of the synagogue called me and said they *really* wanted to
schedule a meeting. When I suggested that a spring meeting, post-gas
shortage, would be more appropriate, he insisted that I could expect

at least 100 people, all of whom were very interested in the JDL. I continued to hesitate until he made the following offer. They had located a gas station near the entrance to the famous Grossinger's Hotel in Liberty, New York, about halfway between Brooklyn and Binghamton, that guaranteed they would be open and have gas available. At my destination in Binghamton, they would have gas ready to refill my car. I finally agreed to accept the speaking engagement, despite my wife's protestations that I was meshugga (crazy). I had a very enjoyable and successful evening, although I really wanted to check into Grossinger's in order to shorten my return trip home. The trip was worthwhile, as I brought back a nice check for the JDL and met some committed Jews living in the hinterlands.

In November 1974, world events brought the JDL back into the spotlight when PLO leader and chief terrorist, Yasser Arafat, was invited to address the United Nations. Jewish organizations and many politicians vehemently opposed Arafat entering the United States. Despite all the opposition, the United States State Department granted Arafat permission to enter the United States and address the United Nations General Assembly. As almost all mainstream Jewish organizations were "up in arms" over the decision to permit this arch-terrorist into America, I did not anticipate that there would be any need for the JDL to get involved.

However, on the morning of November 11, 1974, the day after Arafat's arrival in New York, I received a call from Russel Kelner, operations director of the JDL, asking me about the proximity of my office to the Waldorf Astoria Hotel, where Arafat was reported to be staying. I advised Russ that the Waldorf was one block from my office. Russ then told me that the JDL would like to have a sit-in or other demonstration at the hotel that evening, and he wanted me to see how the police were controlling access to the hotel. At noon, I walked over to the hotel, and, except for three or four of New York City's finest at the entrance, access to the building seemed to be free.

I had no trouble entering the hotel and the lobby. No one would have known that an arch-terrorist was staying at the hotel. I returned to my office and reported my experience back to Russ.

"Of course," I said to Russ, "I was by myself and in business attire. I could not guarantee that there would be such easy access if five or more JDL youths with banners and flags tried to enter the hotel. Entry might have been a bit more difficult."

The next day, the newspapers reported that Arafat was not staying in the Waldorf Astoria. Rather, he was staying at the Waldorf Towers, around the corner from the main entrance on Park Avenue and in a private suite section of the hotel. If I had tried to enter the hotel on the side of the Waldorf Towers, I am sure that there would have been ample police protection and barricades protecting Arafat when he entered and left the building.

Regardless, I went home after work and did not know what, if anything, transpired at the Waldorf that evening.

When I awoke in the morning and turned on the news, the leading story was that Russ Kelner had been arrested in connection with a threat on Arafat's life. I learned that there had been a small demonstration in the early evening in front of the Waldorf Towers. After the demonstration, there was a press conference at the JDL office to protest Arafat's presence in the city, which, at that time, had the largest Jewish population in the world. John Miller, a reporter for WPIX Channel 11, a local TV station located in New York, was assigned to cover the demonstration at the Waldorf Towers. After attending the demonstration, Miller and his film crew were assigned to cover the JDL press conference.

At the press conference, Kelner was seated in military fatigues behind a desk with a .38 caliber pistol in front of him. To Kelner's right sat another man dressed in military fatigues. In response to reporters' incessant questions, a frustrated Kelner finally said that there was a JDL plot to assassinate Arafat before he left New York.

The film crew for WPIX filmed general shots of the press conference without sound and then proceeded to film John Miller's questioning of Kelner with sound. The transcript of this portion is provided below.

> Kelner: *We have people who have been trained and who are out now and who intend to make sure that Arafat and his lieutenants do not leave this country alive.*
> Miller: *How do you plan to do that? You're going to kill him?*
> Kelner: *I'm talking about justice. I'm talking about equal rights under the law, a law that may not exist, but should exist.*
> Miller: *Are you saying that you plan to kill them?*
> Kelner: *We are planning to assassinate Mr. Arafat…just the way any other murderer is treated.*
> Miller: *Do you have the people picked out for this? Have you planned it out? Have you started this operation?*
> Kelner: *Everything is planned in detail.*
> Miller: *Do you think it will come off?*
> Kelner: *It's going to come off.*
> Miller: *Can you elaborate on where or when or how you plan to take care of this?*
> Kelner: *If I elaborate, it might be a problem in bringing it off.*

Following the interview, Miller and his film crew returned to the WPIX studios, where the film was shown in its entirety on the ten o'clock news. WPIX, whose broadcast signal had a range of 50 miles from its New York City studio on East 42nd Street, was viewed by viewers in New Jersey and Connecticut. The next morning, Kelner was arrested pursuant to the provision of 18USC875(c), which provides as follows: "Whoever transmits in interstate or foreign commerce any communication containing any threat to kidnap any person or any threat to injure the person of another, shall be fined under this title or imprisoned not more than five years, or both." He was arrested for violation of this above law on the basis that when WPIX played the Kelner–Miller interview, there was a transmission by Kelner of a threat to Arafat that fell into the category of "interstate commerce" because the WPIX signal reached New Jersey.

Kelner later told me that he only boasted about the plans to kill Arafat after reporters ignored his responses to incessant questions about the JDL's plans for Arafat. He said that Arafat was too well guarded to be harmed and finally blurted out his threats to Arafat out of frustration. He pleaded not guilty, and the case went to trial. What intrigued me about the entire process was that all of the newspaper reports about the news conference thought it necessary to point out that Kelner was dressed in military garb and there was a pistol (which was legally licensed) on his desk. These same reporters somehow seemed to miss the point that Arafat came to the United Nations in military fatigues with a gun at his side. I always wondered if Arafat had a license for carrying his weapon, and if not, why he was not arrested for carrying an unlicensed firearm.

As the trial approached, Kelner asked me to testify as a character witness on his behalf, and I readily agreed. On the day of my scheduled testimony, I went to the federal courthouse in lower Manhattan and proceeded to the designated courtroom. As a scheduled witness, I had to wait outside of the courtroom until I was called to testify. When I arrived, the hallway outside the courtroom was packed with JDL kids who wanted to show their support for Kelner by attending the trial, but there were not enough seats in the courtroom for everyone. While I waited in their midst to be called to testify, Vincent M., the FBI agent for whom my father-in-law stood at attention when he called the house and with whom I'd had substantial dealings with during the Hurok investigation, came over to me to say hello. I had not seen Vincent in a long time.

I asked him what he was doing there, and he told me that he was a witness for the government. "What could you be testifying on in this matter?" I asked him. Vincent told me that he was the "complaining citizen" who'd heard the threat in New Jersey, thereby establishing that the threat had been transmitted across state lines. Upon hearing this, I exploded. "I thought that investigating JDL activities was just an assignment, so I was comfortable being sociable with you." I continued, practically shouting in his face, all the while in the presence of the JDL members waiting outside the courtroom. "But now I see you are the resident anti-Semite eager to act against the JDL. Do not ever talk to me again except in an official capacity." The spectators in the hallway were stunned at my outburst, and I received a round of applause from them. Vincent walked away in silence, and I do not recall ever seeing him again. At last, my name was called, and I entered the courtroom prepared to be a character witness for Kelner.

A character witness is a person who testifies on behalf of a defendant's reputation for honesty and morality — both by personal knowledge of the witness and the person's reputation in the community. I never believed that character witness testimony was useful; I considered it neutral at best. Despite my reservations, I was not going to refuse Kelner, as I genuinely liked him and thought he was dedicated to the Jewish people. After affirming that my testimony was the truth, I stated my credentials, which included possessing a Juris Doctor degree from Brooklyn Law School and a Master of Law (in Taxation) from New York University Law School. I also testified that I was a frequent speaker on behalf of the JDL and spoke in many communities in the New York area. When taking questions about the JDL during my visits to these varied communities, I often heard the audience express complimentary views about Kelner.

After I completed my testimony, the United States Attorney decided to cross-examine me. Believing that my testimony would have absolutely no impact on the jury's decision in the case, I could not understand why they would bother with cross-examination. I thought that declining to cross-examine me would be his way of showing the jury the limited value of character witness testimony. The peril of calling a character witness for the defense is that on cross-examination, the character of the witness can be challenged by the prosecution, and if the witness is not "squeaky clean," their cross-examination could be a difficult ordeal.

Thus, the prosecuting attorney proceeded to try and impugn my character, wanting to know if I was, by virtue of being admitted to practice law in New York, an officer of the court. After affirming my commitment to uphold the law in my capacity as a practicing attorney, I was then asked how I could testify on behalf of Kelner, a person who threatened to kill Yasser Arafat. I responded by saying that I believed in the teachings of the Jewish Talmud, which states, "If someone comes to slay you, slay him first." With that, the courtroom burst out in cheers and applause, with some members actually giving me a standing ovation. The judge was banging his gavel furiously, threatening to clear the courtroom unless quiet was restored. When quiet was finally restored, I was dismissed with an angry glare from the United States Attorney.

While I was not expecting to be cross-examined, I was even more surprised that the questioning of me and the three other character witnesses who testified on Kelner's behalf was one of the areas brought up on appeal by Kelner's appellate lawyer. The appeals judge held that the cross-examination was proper, and even if it had not been, any error in the cross-examination was not a basis for overturning Kelner's conviction. I viewed this language of the appeals court as confirming my belief that character witness testimony is not relevant to the outcome of the trial.

The night after my testimony, I was asked to come to the JDL office to review a transcript of my testimony, as Kelner's lawyer had only 24 hours to request a change in the transcript if there were any errors. When I entered the office, I was treated with great respect, as my exploits, both outside the courtroom and on the stand, were being recounted by those who had been in attendance to those who had not been.

As I expected, my testimony had little effect on the jury, who found Kelner guilty. Kelner was sentenced to a one-year suspended sentence, which was probably the judge's way of saying that the Kelner prosecution was wasting time and money trying the case. Despite the suspended sentence, Kelner appealed his conviction on several grounds, with his case argued by the eminent constitutional lawyer Nathan Lewin. Nevertheless, his conviction was upheld.

It's been many years since the Kelner trial, and due to most of the incidents related here, I had not thought about it for over 40 years. Then, two years ago, while watching the Women's January 17, 2017 March on Washington on TV in Israel, an event occurred that brought back the memory of the trial. Madonna, a world pop music icon, was called to the podium. Addressing the crowd, Madonna said, "Yes, I am angry. Yes, I am outraged. Yes, I have thought an awful lot about blowing up the White House." Madonna's remarks, broadcast around the world, certainly constituted interstate commerce. In addition to falling under the provisions of the same statute according to which Kelner was tried and convicted, Madonna also violated statutes 18USC871 that makes it a crime to threaten the life of the President of the United States. Despite many calls for her arrest, Madonna was never charged with a crime and was even the subject of numerous op-ed pieces proclaiming her innocence.

Interestingly enough, many of Madonna's supporters cited the same reasons that Nathan Lewin raised on appeal for Kelner. Nevertheless, Madonna was never charged, while Kelner was found guilty. On appeal, Mr. Lewin argued that Kelner did not "cause" the transmission of a communication in interstate commerce within the meaning of the statute, because his alleged threat was made in the context of a TV news interview, and it was the wholly independent conduct of the

TV station that resulted in the film of the interview being broadcast across state lines. The second basis for the appeal was that there had been no "communication" within the statute because there was no specific addressee of the alleged threat. Kelner could not have been expecting Arafat to be watching Channel 11; that is to say, he was not expecting Arafat to watch the WPIX ten o'clock news. Moreover, there was no evidence that the "threat" actually reached Arafat. Lewin's third claim was that there was no communication "in interstate commerce" within the statute because even though WPIX televised beyond the borders of New York, the communication did not have to cross state lines to travel from Kelner to Arafat. The fourth claim was that the statements made were not "threats" within the meaning of the statute because Kelner had no intention of actually using force, and the statements were only "political hyperbole." Other than anti-Semitism on behalf of the Justice Department, I really could not understand why Kelner was charged and convicted and Madonna was never even charged with a crime.

JEWISH TELEGRAPHIC AGENCY
July 11, 1975

JDL Leader Fined $1000 for
Threatening to Kill Arafat

Russel Kelner, national coordinator of the Jewish Defense League, was fined $1000 yesterday and put on four years' probation for threatening to kill Palestine Liberation Organization leader Yasir Arafat last November. Federal Judge Richard Owens, who also gave Kelner a one-year suspended jail sentence, said he was giving the JDL official the benefit of the doubt, because he did not mean to carry out the threat. Kelner made the threat during a televised news conference just prior to Arafat's appearance at the United Nations. He was convicted last month by a Manhattan federal court jury. The maximum penalty is five years in prison and a $1000 fine.

- 27 -

THE PLOT THICKENS

OLLOWING MY TESTIMONY IN THE Kelner trial, my activity
on behalf of the JDL was limited to making speeches on their
behalf. With Rabbi Kahane then living in Israel, my active
participation in defending JDL members was apparently no longer
required.

In 1971, Rabbi Kahane pleaded guilty to a firearms charge and was
sentenced to five years' probation. As a condition of his probation,
Rabbi Kahane was ordered not to engage in any activities involving
firearms or any other activities for which Kahane and the JDL had
become known. With Kahane living in Israel and becoming more
active on the Israeli political scene, it was only a matter of time before
he would engage in activities that, if performed in the United States,
would have been a violation of the terms of his probation. However,
as long as he stayed in Israel, he was outside of the jurisdiction of the
Federal District Court, and he could not be punished by the United
States for his activities.

Nevertheless, in 1975 Kahane planned a trip to the United States.
As best as I recall, his visit was more in the nature of fundraising,
as he planned to embark on a speaking tour. Kahane's position was
that the probation restrictions placed on him in 1971 applied to the
United States only, whereas there was concern that Judge Weinstein
intended his probation requirements to be worldwide. Despite concern

that he would be arrested for violating his probation if he returned to the United States, Kahane nevertheless returned — and with great fanfare; many of his followers were waiting at the airport to greet him. Following his return, he was arrested and brought before Judge Weinstein. Kahane admitted that he had violated the terms of his probation and then told Judge Weinstein, "Do what you have to do with a clear conscience. I did what I had to do with a clear conscience." Judge Weinstein sentenced Rabbi Kahane to one year in prison, declaring that the Rabbi had twice "willfully and intentionally" violated the terms of his probation. Kahane served his sentence in a halfway house in Manhattan and was permitted to leave the premises during daylight hours.

During this time, I met with him on numerous occasions, as he wanted me to assist a Jewish family from Tunisia who resided on the lower floors of the building that served as a welfare hotel and halfway house for certain prisoners. The family had several issues with Social Security and the New York City Welfare Board, and they needed someone to help them. For whatever reason — call it his charisma, his sincerity, or just a belief in the inherent goodness of the man — I took on the case (pro bono, of course) and spent the next three years obtaining equity for the family. Their initial argument with Social Security concerned a $100 a month cut in the SSI allotment for the father. The family consisted of four members, and their combined monthly income was approximately $1200, of which $900 went toward their rent, leaving just $300 for food for four people. After a three-year battle with Social Security and several administrative hearings, an administrative judge awarded the family $15,000, which was more money than these people could have imagined. In gratitude, they offered me 50% of the award. When I refused any payment, they were ecstatic and set for life.

On the afternoon of January 24, 1975, while in my office, I heard on the radio that a bomb had exploded at Fraunces Tavern, killing 4 people and injuring more than 50 others. One of the oldest buildings in New York, the Tavern served as George Washington's headquarters during the American Revolution, and it was also the site of peace negotiations between the Americans and the British. Later, this historic building was converted into an upscale restaurant and private dining club.

The Puerto Rican clandestine paramilitary organization "Fuerzas Armadas de Liberación Nacional Puertorriqueña" (the Armed Forces of Puerto Rican National Liberation, or FALN), which had set off other bombs in New York in the 1970s, claimed responsibility for the bombing. New Yorkers were in a frenzy as fear of additional bombings gripped the city, and police were under tremendous pressure to catch the bombers before another bomb exploded. A group of concerned citizens offered a reward of $50,000 (an exorbitant sum in 1975; today's value would be the equivalent of a reward of nearly $250,000) for any information that led to the arrest and conviction of the bombers. Anyone with information was urged to call the telephone number that was continually flashed on the television screen. That is when it became relevant to my story.

- 28 -

ANOTHER MYSTERIOUS
PHONE CALL

AT SOME POINT IN THIS frenzy, I received a call from an individual who introduced himself only as "Saul." I asked him
whether I knew him, and Saul said that I did not. With my
curiosity aroused, I asked him what I could do for him. Saul told me
that while he was not a member of the JDL, he had many friends who
were active members. He further explained that he needed a lawyer
who could be trusted with a delicate assignment. When he'd asked
his JDL friends for the name of a lawyer who could be trusted, my
name came up many times, so he decided to seek my help.

I was curious as to the nature of the assignment, and Saul told
me that he might have information about the identity of the FALN
bombers who blew up Fraunces Tavern.

"That's great," I said. "You should call the hotline on TV, and if
your information is correct, you could get a $50,000 reward."

"I am not interested in any reward," he answered.

"Well, what is it that you want from me?"

Saul then explained what he wanted me to do. Although he was not
a JDL member, he was a big fan of Rabbi Kahane, who, at that time, was
sitting in his halfway house serving time for his parole violation. Saul
proceeded to explain that he would only come forward and give the

police whatever information he had in exchange for the release of Rabbi Kahane. If his information was of value, then, in lieu of the reward, he wanted Rabbi Kahane to be released from confinement. If his information did not aid in the capture of the bombers, then the Rabbi would remain under arrest. My assignment was to negotiate a deal whereby Rabbi Kahane would be released in exchange for Saul's information.

Before I could accept the assignment, I explained to Saul that I would need to meet with him and get a sense of whether he was for real or just some crackpot who, if I proceeded with his assignment, would prove embarrassing to me. After all, if his information was correct, he would be entitled to a $50,000 reward. In order to protect Saul's identity, I set up the following ground rules. First, anticipating that I would be pressured to disclose his name without his agreement, I did not want to know Saul's last name, place of residence, or telephone number. Second, I instructed him to call me whenever he wanted to get an update. As a result of my first condition, I would not know how to contact him. Saul agreed to these conditions, and we parted.

Two days later, on a rainy Sunday morning, I drove to my office across from the Waldorf Astoria Hotel and proceeded to call the hotline number that I had copied down from the television screen the night before.

"New York City Bomb Squad," was the reply. "Detective Parola speaking."

At first, the name did not register with me, and in response to how he could help me, I proceeded to explain the reason for my call.

"My name is Arthur Miller, and I am an attorney representing a client who may have information concerning the identities of the perpetrators of the Fraunces Tavern bombing."

Before I could explain further, he said, "Art, this is Sam. Don't you remember me from the Siegel case?"

I replied in the affirmative and then proceeded to explain the situation. What my unnamed client wanted was to exchange his information for Rabbi Kahane release, if it turned out that his information was valuable. Detective Parola responded that the police were under tremendous pressure from the Mayor of New York to solve the case. Parola said that if it were up to him, he would let Rabbi Kahane go free in a heartbeat if it would get the FALN bombers off the streets before another blast. The problem was that Rabbi Kahane was in the federal judicial system, and New York City did not have any jurisdiction or power to make any agreement with respect to releasing the Rabbi. Sam did say, however, that he would contact the federal authorities, explain the substance of our telephone conversation, and tell them how to contact me. Then, he made a simple request for making the connection between me and the feds.

"If anything comes from your information and the feds call a news conference to announce the arrest, you must agree to call me so that my captain and I can be on the podium."

My mind immediately went to the numerous times I had seen police press conferences where it looked like every police officer even remotely involved in a case was squeezing onto the podium smiling for the cameras.

"Sam, you have my word that I will keep you informed."

The next morning, I received a phone call from someone who identified himself as a special agent from the FBI, inviting me to come to the FBI's New York offices that afternoon to meet with the agent and a representative of the United States Attorney's office in order to discuss my conversation with Detective Sam Parola of the day before. At this time, I really thought that my request was a "no-brainer." Rabbi Kahane was in a halfway house with freedom to roam the city until nightfall, and in exchange for his full freedom, I could give them information that would get the bombers off the streets before another blast.

The FBI agent asked me who this witness was, and I replied that I did not know anything about him except for his first name, which

I would not reveal until I had a signed agreement that Rabbi Kahane would be released from jail if our information led to the arrest of the FALN bombers. The agent and the attorney indicated that neither of them was high enough in the power structure to enter into such an agreement and that they needed to consult with their superiors.

"We will get back to you just as soon as a decision is made."

"What is there to decide?" I responded. "I am willing to trade information about the most wanted people in New York in exchange for letting Rabbi Kahane go free and return home to Israel."

I expected to hear them say that I was right, but they merely repeated their prior comment: "We will get back to you."

- 29 -

THE SILENCE CONTINUES

THE NEXT MORNING, SAUL CALLED me at my office, and I brought him up to date on all that had transpired since I last met him. I informed him that I was awaiting a response to our request from either the FBI or the United States Attorney. I had no idea how long that would take, but I told Saul that with all the pressure on the law enforcement agencies, I was expecting an answer quite soon. I was so confident that the feds had to agree with my proposal that I began drafting an agreement between all the parties so that as soon as the FBI called me, I would have the agreement ready for signature.

The first week went by with not a word back from the authorities. By the second week, still waiting for a response, I started to become concerned. I could not believe that keeping Rabbi Kahane in a halfway house for the remainder of his year-long sentence was more important than getting these terrorists behind bars, where they belonged. When Saul called me during the second week, I told him that I was considering putting pressure on the government by going to the press. I felt that the newspapers or television reporters would be outraged if they knew that the government was not acting on our request to exchange information regarding the identity of the Fraunces Tavern terrorists for Rabbi Kahane's release.

As a concerned citizen, I was afraid that another deadly bomb would go off while the government was procrastinating. Saul and I decided to give it a few more days before we contacted the press. I was in my office on Wednesday when I received a phone call from my receptionist advising me that a United States marshal was in the lobby and wanted to see me. Not knowing what was happening, I cautiously went to the lobby and saw the marshal there. I quickly went to him and asked him why he wanted to see me. My first thought was that he had to be mistaken and had the wrong person by the same name.

The marshal did not respond to my question as to whether he had the right party. Instead, he proceeded to hand me a subpoena demanding my appearance before a federal grand jury in lower Manhattan the following morning. Once again, I inquired as to whether there was a mistake, but he said there was no mistake. In a loud voice that everyone in the reception area could hear, he said I should be prepared to give testimony in the matter of the Fraunces Tavern bombing. I cannot describe the stares of the people in the lobby when he mentioned the Fraunces Tavern bombing, as everyone wondered what my involvement in this matter was.

- 30 -

THE GRAND JURY

THE RULES OF THE GRAND jury provide that a lawyer is not permitted to be in the grand jury room while his client is being questioned. If the client has a question about how to respond, he simply informs the government attorney examining him (there is no judge in the grand jury room) and asks to be excused in order to consult his attorney, who sits patiently outside the grand jury room. While this system provides the witness access to his lawyer, it is not the same as if the lawyer is inside the grand jury room. A person excusing himself to consult his lawyer requires the witness to recognize when he needs consultation with his lawyer. In most instances during a trial, it is the lawyer who recognizes the danger of or admissibility of a particular question and either objects to it or asks to speak with his client.

As I had never testified before a grand jury, I expected my entire testimony to last just a few minutes. After all, in my mind, I possessed no information about the Fraunces Tavern bombing that I had not told the FBI and the United States attorney in my request to obtain the release of Rabbi Kahane. As I was called into the grand jury room, I entered full of confidence, with little concern about what was going to happen. As I entered, I saw that my old nemesis, Henry Putzel, was conducting the examination. We greeted each other, and I sat down in the witness chair.

The first few questions were nothing more than me giving my name, address, education background, and so on. Henry then asked me if I had any knowledge about the Fraunces Tavern bombing. I told him that I had no direct knowledge, but I had a client who might have some useful information. In response to Henry's questions, I then retold the entire story about Saul contacting me and my meeting with the FBI, concluding with my amazement that nearly two weeks after my first contact with Detective Parola, I was still awaiting an answer from the government. Hoping for Putzel to express the same sense of outrage at the government's delay in accepting our offer that I was feeling, I did not expect his next question.

"What is the name of your client?'

I responded that I did not know his full name, only his first name.

In response to further questions, I related that I had to wait for my client to call me, as I had no knowledge as to how to contact him.

"And what is his first name?" came Henry's next question.

"I cannot answer that question as to his identity because of attorney-client privilege," I responded.

Attorney-client privilege is a rule of law designed to encourage frank and open communications between a lawyer and his client. If there is any written or oral communication between a lawyer and his client, then the lawyer can neither disclose nor be forced to disclose the substance of the communication. In order for a communication to be "privileged," four elements are required: There must be a communication between privileged persons, and it must be made in confidence for the purpose of seeking, obtaining, or providing legal assistance to the client.

Henry appeared to relish my answer and quickly responded, "The identity of your client is not within attorney-client privilege. Now, I ask you once again, what is his first name?"

"I disagree with you. The name of *your* client may not be a privileged communication, but when the very essence of the communication is his identity, then I believe it is covered by attorney–client privilege."

Putzel then explained to the grand jurors that when a witness refuses to answer a question, he must be taken before a judge, and, if the judge determines that the question is a proper question, then the witness must either answer the question or be held in contempt of court. If the judge finds the witness in contempt of court, he will be arrested and will sit in jail until he either answers the question or the grand jury session ends. Putzel then told the grand jurors that there would be a recess in the proceedings, as I would be brought before a judge in order to compel me to testify.

Obviously, this was not the way I was expecting my morning to go. Suddenly faced with the possibility of being held in contempt of court, I requested that I be given the right to meet with an attorney. Putzel quickly responded to my request with "Oh, come on, Arthur, you are an attorney. You have no need to consult with one now and delay these proceedings." I could not think of any reason for his comments besides anti-Semitism. My response was probably not what he was expecting. I shouted back at him, "I resent any attempt to deprive me of my right to counsel. Do I detect a hint of anti-Semitism in your response?" I was tempted to respond with the old adage that a lawyer who represents himself has a fool for a client. What does it say about the lawyer who recommends to another lawyer that he should represent himself?

Putzel did not respond; rather, he said we should go down to the ninth floor, where a judge was waiting for us. We entered the courtroom, interrupting whatever proceedings were going on at the time, and Putzel explained the situation to the judge. I then responded by stating my position that under these circumstances the client's name was covered by attorney-client privilege. Furthermore, I needed time to consult my attorney. I further explained that I had no knowledge or reason to know that I would be a target facing imprisonment that morning; therefore, I had not consulted or even obtained my own lawyer.

The judge stated that he was not about to find someone in contempt of court in a case in which the recalcitrant witness had requested his right to counsel. Besides, he was intrigued by the novel question I raised. He then adjourned my appearance and told both Putzel and me to return on Monday prepared to argue my position. The judge reminded me that he would not grant me any extension, so I should not waste time in obtaining counsel. I was excused from further testimony and now had only three days to obtain counsel. I definitely followed the judge's advice.

- 31 -

JACOB EVSAROFF
TO THE RESCUE

FOLLOWING THE JUDGE'S RULING THAT I had to obtain counsel and return to his courtroom on Monday morning, I hurried back to my office to make a few phone calls. My first call was to Hyman Dechter, an attorney who had begun to handle JDL cases over the last year or two. I related all of the proceedings to Hy and told him that I really needed a top lawyer who I could meet as soon as possible. He said he would get back to me in an hour or two. In fact, he called me within the hour, saying he had consulted with Jacob (Jack) Evsaroff, one of the top criminal attorneys in New York. Jack was intrigued by the issues I had raised. Hy told me that I had an appointment with Jack at his Brooklyn office at 11 a.m. the following morning. Moreover, since he was certainly interested in any case that would expand attorney-client privilege, he agreed that he would not charge me for his representation. I was very relieved that I had a strong legal backing for my case.

When I returned home, Saul called me to find out if there had been any further developments, as was his practice on Thursday night. I explained everything that had transpired with the grand jury and my scheduled appearance the next Monday morning. Much to his credit, Saul said that he never intended for me to be facing contempt of court charges and that he was now willing to come in and speak to the FBI to tell them all he knew about the possible identity of the bombers. I told him that it was his decision to make, but I saw no reason why we couldn't wait until Monday morning. If the judge agreed with me that his identity was privileged, then there was no reason for him to come forward without an agreement concerning Rabbi Kahane.

I further explained that I was becoming quite angry at the refusal of the government to negotiate with us. Everyone, lawyers and laymen alike, knows that law enforcement authorities often free dangerous criminals in exchange for testimony that could doom another criminal. As an example, I referred Saul to the Amtorg and Hurok cases, in which the government was willing to grant immunity in these bombings to the man who made the bombs. Therefore, I told Saul that I was beginning to think that there had to be a reason, such as anti-Semitism, why the rabbi was being held to a harsher standard. I concluded that I was willing to play out this whole process, including being held in contempt of court, to expose it.

Finally, I told Saul to call me before Shabbat and I would bring him up to date on my meeting with Mr. Evsaroff. Saul then made a rather startling admission, telling me that if things did not go well with my lawyer and I needed to speak to him, he had written his telephone number on page 1275 of the Bronx telephone directory that was in my office. I did not really want to know this information, recognizing that if I was ordered by the judge to disclose my client's identity, I could satisfy the judge's order just by giving Saul's name. Whether this was enough information for the FBI to track him down, I did not know. I was sure the FBI would be able to find him, but how long it would take would be another matter. Now that I had knowledge of his phone number, once I disclosed the information, finding Saul would be a simple matter.

I then thought that it was time to explain my legal issues and the possibility of my arrest to my wife. I told her that I believed there was an underlying level of anti-Semitism behind what was transpiring, and if that was the case, I was willing to make this fact public — even if I had to go to jail. I tried to calm her fears by saying that after my meeting with my lawyer on Friday morning, I was considering going to the press and letting them know that the federal government was more interested in keeping Rabbi Kahane in a halfway house than in releasing him in exchange for information on the Fraunces Tavern bombing. Needless to say, I had a sleepless night as I planned my next move.

- 32 -

AN EVENTFUL
FRIDAY MORNING

I ARRIVED AT MY OFFICE ON Friday morning around 8 a.m. to get some work done before my 11 a.m. meeting with Jack Evsaroff. At 8:30 a.m., the phone rang. It was a very angry Detective Sam Parola on the phone.

"Art, how could you do this to me? I thought we had a deal. I kept my part of the bargain and put you in touch with the feds."

"Slow down a little. Sam, I have no idea what you are talking about."

"The word downtown is that the feds have called a news conference for noon to announce an arrest in the Fraunces Tavern bombing," he shouted at me.

"Sam, if there is going to be an arrest in the case, I had nothing to do with it. In fact, I am supposed to return to the grand jury on Monday, and the judge will rule whether my client's identity is a privileged communication."

Sam said that this was not consistent with the rumors downtown. He also said his captain was more than annoyed that they had not been invited to the press conference. I repeated that I was not involved in any information that would lead to an arrest in the case. After going back and forth with Detective Parola for several more minutes, he

128

calmed down, convinced that I had not reneged on our deal. He said he would get to the bottom of the rumors circulating at police head-quarters. The phone rang ten minutes later, and I grabbed it quickly, hoping that the confusion with Detective Parola had been resolved.

Detective Parola told me what he'd found out: The FBI had called a press conference for noon, at which time they were going to announce *my* arrest in the case. Moreover, television reporters were going to accompany FBI agents to my office to film my arrest. Again, I said there must have been a mistake. I had until Monday to appear before a judge. In fact, I told Sam, I had an 11 a.m. meeting that day with my lawyer to discuss Monday's strategy. Detective Parola responded that he was just reporting what he had found out, and if I did not want to be arrested at my office, I should be someplace else before noon. In a panic, I called Jack Evsaroff and reported to him the substance of what Parola had told me. Jack suggested that I come to his office immediately and he would try to find out what was happening.

Before I left my office, I went into the office of Paul Bodner, who was the partner-in-charge of my department to let him now that there was a strong possibility that I would be the subject of a major story on the news and that I would probably be in jail before the day was out. Although Paul observed very little of our religion (I cannot even recall if he worked on Yom Kippur), he was one of four people who did whatever they could to ensure that I was treated solely based on my performance and not based on my religious observance. As a result, I wanted to prepare him for what might happen, knowing that he could be under pressure if I was arrested, and I did not want him to be unprepared for any fallout. I also went to page 1275 of the Bronx phone book and copied Saul's number in case I needed to discuss anything with him.

As the subway train transported me to downtown Brooklyn, my resolve to see these developments to their logical conclusion increased with each stop of the train. The more I thought about what had transpired, I knew that anti-Semitic forces in the government were behind the developments, and I became determined to stand up against this discrimination, regardless of the consequences.

I arrived at Evsaroff's office a little after 10 a.m. My heart raced, as I was tried to plan what I would do in response to the threats I faced. With shaking hands, I entered the Evsaroff Law Offices, where Jack waited for me at reception. As we entered his office, he called in one of his associates to sit in on the meeting. Before I had a chance to speak, the associate said that he had been doing research on the issue of whether a client's name could be considered privileged communication. He said that he had not found any New York case law on the subject, but he had found a case in the Midwest where there was very favorable language supporting the existence of the privilege. There were two problems, however, with the decision. First, it was not a New York case, so a federal judge sitting in New York would not be bound by the decision. Second, the favorable language was dicta. Dicta, or obiter dictum, is a Latin phrase that literally means "that which is said in passing." In legal usage, it refers to a statement made by a judge in his or her opinion that was not necessary for the judge to reach his conclusion. If this decision was the only precedent we could cite on Monday, it was doubtful that the judge would give it much weight in his decision.

Jack thanked the associate for his meticulous research but told him that a new problem had arisen. I then proceeded to relate all of the events of the last two weeks, including the details of my telephone conversations with Detective Parola of that morning. I told Jack that my client was willing to speak to the FBI in order to keep me from having to go to jail, but I was not ready to let him come in. I explained that as I believed that the government's reluctance to agree to Rabbi Kahane's release, the way I was treated by the United States Attorney, and their decision to ignore the judge's ruling to give me until Monday to return before the judge all pointed to a certain degree of anti-Semitism. I then told him that I thought it was time to go public with what had transpired. I thought that the public would be as outraged as I was if they knew the federal government was more intent on arresting me and keeping Rabbi Kahane in his halfway house than agreeing to his release if Saul's information proved correct. If we were going to go public, I thought it would be important to do so prior to the noon press conference and certainly before the FBI and the TV cameras came to my office. "Finally," I said, "if all else fails and I am not due in court until Monday, I could always disappear for the weekend."

Jack said that before we considered these options, I should give him a few minutes to make a phone call and let him see what the situation was. He told me that he was going to call the head of the FBI's New York office, who was a friend of his. I have to admit that knowing my lawyer could call the head of the FBI directly and was on a first-name basis with him gave me an enormous amount of comfort. I could only hear Jack's side of the conversation (speakerphones were not in vogue in 1975). Thus, my version of the conversation went something like this:

Jack told the FBI chief what I had reported to him, and apparently the chief replied that what I said was accurate and that a news conference was called for noon, when I was scheduled to be arrested. Jack then told the FBI chief that the most important thing was that the FBI and the TV cameras not go to my office, as I was no longer there. Rather, I was sitting in Jack's office. Jack further assured the FBI that I would stay in his office until the matter had been resolved and that, regardless of what had transpired, in the next few hours, I recognized that I was still under subpoena to return to the grand jury on Monday. I was not a flight risk.

That was not completely true, as Ronnie and I had discussed the possibility of going to Canada before Shabbat and then flying to Israel from Canada. I'd explained to Ronnie that if I did flee to Israel, being under subpoena, I doubted I would ever be able to return to the United. States. We had ruled out this flight possibility on Thursday night, as it would require Ronnie to assume full responsibility for moving to Israel to join me. However, this had all transpired on Thursday — before I knew what the FBI had in store for me on Friday morning.

Jack then related the controversy over the extent of attorney-client privilege and asked whether it would be more appropriate to wait until after the hearing with the judge. That's when the most shocking admission came out, convincing me that there was an anti-Semitic element behind the events. In response to Jack's suggestion that this matter be put on hold until the judge's ruling on Monday, the head of the FBI's New York office told Jack, "Shots are being called from Washington," and he had no discretion in the matter. Both Jack and I were momentarily in shock when the head of the FBI's New York office, who I assumed was pretty high up in the power structure of the FBI, admitted that he was following orders from Washington. I did get some comfort when he told Jack that he would call off the visit to my office as well as the press conference to give us time to resolve this matter.

Upon hearing that the FBI's National Office in Washington had ordered my arrest, I asked Jack whether he thought there was anti-Semitism involved and whether he agreed that I should fight it. Jack told me that he was my lawyer and that his advice, which I was free to accept or not, was to stay out of jail. I could always contact the press after the threat to my personal freedom had been resolved. I then told Jack that as of that morning, I had Saul's telephone number, and I wanted to discuss this with him further. I called Saul, and, fortunately, he was home. I related the situation to him and reiterated, "I am prepared to go to jail if you do not want me to give your information to the FBI." Saul said that under no conditions should I allow myself to be arrested on his behalf. He told me that he would be in Jack's office by 1:30 p.m. and that he would meet with the FBI to give them whatever information he had. I gave Saul a chance to reconsider, but he said he was already on his way out the door.

After I relayed the substance of my conversation with Saul, Jack assured me that we were both doing the right thing. Jack called the FBI chief and told him that my client was on his way to Jack's office, and he requested an extension of my arrest until 2 p.m., to which the FBI agreed. Two FBI agents came to Jack's office to await Saul's arrival and to babysit me in order to make sure I didn't run off in the event that Saul was a no-show. In fact, Saul arrived before 1:30 p.m., and I introduced him to the FBI agents. I was then told that it was okay for me to leave and that my appearance at the grand jury on Monday was no longer required. I breathed a sigh of relief. I thanked Jack profusely for what he had done on my behalf, and I told Saul, "Well, if your information is good, we can always put in for the $50,000 reward." I went home, told my wife the good news, and proceeded to spend a wonderful, carefree Shabbat.

On Monday, I realized that I had not received the $40 witness fee plus $5 for transportation costs for my Thursday morning appearance before the grand jury. Several weeks went by, and still I had not received my $45. I was upset, but not because I needed the $45. I was upset because after all of the needless aggravation that the government caused me and knowing that an apology from Putzel would never come, I believed that I had really earned that fee. I picked up the phone to call Henry Putzel and tell him I was still waiting for my check but decided against it. It was better to leave well enough alone and not reopen any sore wounds he may feel toward me. By the way, it is 2020, and I am still waiting for my check.

- 33 -
ANTI-SEMITISM

IN THE INTRODUCTION TO THIS book, I explained that I made the decision to tell my story after certain incidents suggested to me that the treatment of Jonathan Pollard was the result of anti-Semitism at the highest levels of the government, which reminded me of the events of 1975 when I became wanted by the FBI. Jonathan Pollard, who admitted to an act of espionage for a friendly country, entered into a plea bargain in exchange for his admission of guilt. Despite the almost universally accepted practice of judges to respect a plea agreement between the defendant and the government, the Pollard plea agreement was ignored by the sentencing judge. Instead of the expected prison sentence of a few years, the judge sentenced Pollard to life imprisonment.

Why?

Apparently, the plea agreement was ignored by the trial judge following receipt of a document from Secretary of Defense Caspar Weinberger. The Weinberger Memorandum, as the document became known, allegedly addressed the serious damage that Pollard's actions did to the security interests of the United States. So damning was the memorandum that for nearly 30 years of Pollard's imprisonment, the accusations concerning the damage to United States security were always cited as the basis for his continued incarceration. As the years passed and the pleas for Pollard's release grew louder, the contents of the memorandum were cited time and time again as the reason for not granting Pollard his release. Finally, in 2013, after a long battle by Pollard's attorneys to obtain the contents of the memorandum and after Pollard had been in prison for 28 years, parts of the memorandum were finally released.

An analysis of the document and other correspondence related to the Pollard issue showed that the supposed accusations against Pollard in the memorandum were lies. The falsified details of the memorandum supported my belief of anti-Semitism in the upper echelons of the federal government. At the time of his sentencing and in the nearly 30 years that has elapsed since then, the government has continually maintained that Pollard did great harm to the United States' national security. As the years went by and as contradictory documents were released, the government continued to maintain its claim about the damage to national security resulting from the materials Pollard passed on to the United States' ally, Israel. The material includes the victim impact statement, a recently declassified 1987 CIA damage assessment of the case, and now, the new declassifications of the Weinberger document itself.

In 2013, after he had been in prison for over 28 years, Pollard was finally granted a parole hearing. The government continued to oppose granting Pollard's parole, once again citing what had now become a discredited Weinberger memorandum. Nevertheless, the parole board accepted the government's characterization of the Weinberger memorandum without actually reviewing the now declassified document.

Officials who have reviewed the majority of the memorandum (20% of the memorandum was still classified at the time of his first parole hearing) now see that rather than describing Pollard's actions as damaging to the security of the United States, the document charges that Pollard's activities affected the United States' relationships with Middle Eastern countries. Weinberger believed that the damage done to US-Arab relations was detrimental to the security interests of the

United States, which is a far cry from the generally accepted under-standing of the Weinberger memorandum as showing that the damage to US security justified life imprisonment.

Eliot Lauer and Jacques Semmelman, partners in the prestigious law firm of Curtis, Mallet-Prevost, Colt & Mosle LLP who represented Pollard in obtaining the release of the memorandum, stated that "the recent disclosures…show that the government has been dishonestly hiding behind the mask of 'classified information' to materially mis-characterize the nature and extent of the harm caused by Mr. Pollard."

Even Weinberger, in an interview in 2002, four years prior to his death, stated that the Pollard affair was "a very minor matter. It was made far bigger than its actual importance." Why was he silent all those years? Robert C. McFarlane served as United States National Security Adviser when Caspar Weinberger was Secretary of Defense. In 2012, McFarlane wrote, "The affidavit filed by former Secretary of Defense Caspar Weinberger was surely inspired in large part by his deeply held animus toward the State of Israel. His extreme bias against Israel was manifested in recurrent episodes of strong crit-icism and unbalanced reasoning when decisions involving Israel were being made." McFarlane described Pollard's long imprisonment as excessive and a great injustice. Assistant Secretary of Defense during Weinberger's term, Dr. Lawrence J. Korb, stated in 2013 that "the severity of Mr. Pollard's sentence appears to be the result of Mr. Weinberger's almost visceral dislike of the impact that Israel has on U.S. foreign policy." In 2012, former CIA director James Woolsey, in support of Pollard's parole application, stated it was time to "free him." Woolsey has oftentimes stated that "anti-Semitism" was a factor in the ongoing incarceration of Pollard. In an op-ed piece in The Wall Street Journal, he urged the administration to "Forget that Pollard is a Jew…pretend he's a Greek- or Korean- or Filipino-American and free him!" Nevertheless, the Parole Board turned down Pollard's first application for parole.

Following such denial, many knowledgeable senior United States officials urged President Obama to correct the injustice of denying parole to Jonathan Pollard. In their letter to President Obama, senior officials stated that "the allegation that Pollard's espionage 'was the greatest compromise of U.S. security to that date' is false; and not supported by any evidence in the public record or the classified file. Yet it was this fiction that the Parole Commission cited to deny parole." The officials continued by noting that the government relied on a "stale, largely discredited, 28-year-old classified memorandum written by former Secretary of Defense Caspar Weinberger" in making its decision. The letter continued:

"Mr. Weinberger himself discounted his original damage assessment of the Pollard case in a 2002 interview...[and] the unreliability of the 1987 Weinberger document was ignored by the Parole Commission.... Denying a man his freedom based on a claim of damage that is patently false while ignoring exculpatory documentary evidence and hiding behind a veil of secret evidence is neither fair nor just, and it simply is not the American way.... We therefore strongly urge you, Mr. President, to tolerate no further delay in rectifying an injustice that has gone on for far too long. We urge you to act expeditiously to commute Mr. Pollard's life sentence to the [more than] 29 years which he has already served."

President Obama refused to intervene. The facts speak for themselves.

EPILOGUE

FOLLOWING MY EXCITING MORNING AT Jack Evsaroff's office, I anxiously called Saul at the conclusion of Shabbat on Saturday evening to find out what had happened. He told me that he met with the FBI agents and gave them what information he had. The FBI thanked him for coming forward with his information, but they had received the same information from another source, and it was a false alarm. Apparently, several Puerto Rican students at the City College of New York, which Saul attended, were routinely bragging about their involvement in the Fraunces Tavern bombing, but it was nothing more than a prank. I never heard from or spoke to Saul again. To this day, I do not even know his last name.

FALN was responsible for over a hundred bombings in New York for over a decade, beginning in the 1970s. Eventually, an explosion at the home of their principal bombmaker led to the arrest of 16 members of the organization, who were charged with attempting to overthrow the United States government. Included in those arrested and sentenced to long prison terms was Oscar López Rivera, the suspected head of FALN.

In 1999, President William Jefferson Clinton offered the prisoners clemency in exchange for their expressions of remorse for their actions. All prisoners, except for Oscar López Rivera, accepted the offer of clemency. López Rivera refused the clemency offer rather than acknowledge remorse for his actions. The generally accepted reasoning behind the grants of clemency by President Clinton was to help his wife, Hillary Rodham Clinton, who was running for the United States Senate representing New York, to garner the support of New York's large Puerto Rican population. Oscar López Rivera, having refused the clemency grant, remained in prison until he was pardoned by President Barack Obama in the last days of his administration. Even after his release, López Rivera did not acknowledge any remorse for his actions. No one was ever charged in the Fraunces Tavern bombing case, which remains unsolved to this date.

Rabbi Meir Kahane served his sentence in the halfway house, and I continued to meet with him to assist the Jewish residents there. Prior to his return to Israel following his release, there was a farewell dinner in his honor. Ronnie and I were invited to attend, and we readily agreed. I also invited my mother Ruth Miller, a"h, who was a tremendous admirer of Rabbi Kahane, to join us. My mother agreed to come with us on the condition that I introduced her to the Rabbi. At the dinner, I brought my mother over to meet Rabbi Kahane. She thanked him for all the work he did on behalf of Soviet Jews, stating that his parents must be very proud of his work. Rabbi Kahane, who was aware of my efforts to get him released, including my willingness to go to jail, thanked my mother for the compliments but told her that not only was he driven to do what he did, he also received much acclaim for it. He told her that she should be prouder of her son, who did so much behind the scenes. My mother asked me what Rabbi Kahane was referring to, but I said it was not necessary for her to know what I did. My mother never knew how close I came to being arrested in connection with the Fraunces Tavern bombing.

In 1978, I was transferred to Worcester, Massachusetts, where the Rabbi came to speak in Worcester twice. When I met him, he said that he had wondered what had happened to me and was relieved to find out that I was okay. In one of his appearances, he spoke at Worcester's very large reform temple, which had a very liberal Rabbi. His speech occurred shortly after the first Lebanese war, and during his talk, he intimated great displeasure with Israeli political and military leaders who exposed Israeli soldiers to extreme danger in order to limit Lebanese casualties. After he concluded his remarks, the temple's Rabbi asked him to clarify one of his remarks. The temple Rabbi said that there must be some confusion because he got the impression that Rabbi Kahane was giving higher value to the life of an Israeli soldier than to the life of a Lebanese soldier. The response was classic Kahane.

"Did I give that impression? Let me see if I can clear up any confusion. I would wipe out the entire country of Lebanon if it would save the life of just one Israeli soldier."

His *ahavat Yisrael*, love for a fellow Jew, was unconditional.

On November 5, 1990, Rabbi Kahane was shot to death in New York City by an Arab gunman. I drove to New York the following afternoon to attend his funeral at the Young Israel of Ocean Parkway in Brooklyn. On my way into New York, I stopped by Yeshiva University in Washington Heights to visit my son David, who was a senior there. When I arrived downstairs, David excused himself from his class to say he was meeting me downstairs and didn't want to keep me waiting, as I was on my way to Rabbi Kahane's funeral. One of David's friends said that I must have been a big follower of the Rabbi and the JDL, since I drove in from Massachusetts to attend the funeral. David said he didn't really know for sure, as he was only around five years old at the time, but he did recall frequent calls late at night when Rabbi Kahane's name or the JDL was mentioned. Well, David, now you know the rest of the story. Let my grandchildren and great-grandchildren know about their grandfather and great-grandfather.

Due to the overflowing crowd, I was not able to gain entry into Young Israel, so I stayed outside among the thousands of people who could not enter the building and had to listen to the proceedings over the loudspeaker. As the Rabbi's casket, draped in an Israeli flag, was carried out to a hearse waiting to transport his body to Jerusalem for burial, I was able to touch it. Rabbi Meir Kahane was 58 years old at the time of his murder. In a tragic twist of fate, his son, Rabbi Binyamin Zev Kahane, and his wife, Talya, were also shot and killed near the Israeli settlement of Ofra, about ten miles from the holy city of Jerusalem, during the Palestinian intifada. Five of the couple's six children were in the van when they were hit by automatic rifle fire. Binyamin (the driver) was killed, and the vehicle lost control and smashed into a wall. His wife, Talya, died in the ambulance on the way to the hospital.

Sylva Zalmanson, the heroic prisoner of Zion, whose "Free Sylva Zalmanson" button I wore for so many years, was released as part of a prisoner exchange after serving five years in a Soviet prison. She emigrated to Israel and is now one of Israel's top artists. President Barack Hussein Obama completed his eight years in office without taking any steps to rectify the injustice done to Jonathan Pollard. Shame on you, President Obama. Except for Rabbi Kahane, I never saw or spoke to any of the key people mentioned in this book again. I have one fervent prayer: I pray that before this book is published, Jonathan Pollard will come home to Israel, and I can greet him. I can, because on September 27, 2004, my wife and I boarded an El Al jet as we made aliyah (emigrated) to Israel.

ADDENDUM

As CALENDAR YEAR 2020, THE year of the pandemic, drew to a close, I received New Year's wishes from so many people all expressing their hopes and prayers that 2020 was behind us and that 2021 would see life return to normal. On the morning of December 30, as I made the final changes before printing, Ronnie came running into my office and announced that "Jonathan Pollard has just landed in Israel." I had just completed my review of the epilogue and thought about my prayer that Jonathan Pollard would come home to Israel before the book was published. Realizing that my prayer had been answered, I recited the *shehecheyanu* blessing as tears rolled down my face. May all our prayers be answered.

APPENDIX

No. 1087
United States Court of Appeals, Second Circuit

United States v. Huss

In United States v. Huss, 482 F.2d 38, 44 (2d Cir. 1973), we extended the applicability of Gelbard to give a trial witness standing to invoke § 3504 upon his claim of illegal surveillance.

Opinion.

Argued June 2, 1973.

Decided June 26, 1973.

Alan M. Dershowitz, Cambridge, Mass. (Harvey A. Silverglate, Norman S. Zalkind, Zalkind Silverglate, Jeanne Baker, Boston, Mass., on the brief), for appellant Seigel.

Arthur H. Miller, Brooklyn, N.Y., for appellant Huss.

Robert P. Leighton, New York City, for appellant Smilow.

Henry Putzel, III, Asst. U.S. Atty. (Paul J. Curran, U.S. Atty., S. D. N.Y. and Joseph Jaffe, Asst. U.S. Atty., on the brief), for appellee.

Appeal from the United States District Court for the Southern District of New York.

Before KAUFMAN, Chief Judge, SMITH, Circuit Judge, and BRYAN, District Judge.

Of the United States District Court for the Southern District of New

York, sitting by designation.

IRVING R. KAUFMAN, Chief Judge:

On January 26, 1972, a bomb exploded in the New York City offices of Columbia Artists Management, Inc., and in the offices of the internationally renowned impresario Sol Hurok, also in New York City. One life was lost, that of Iris Kones, as a result of these senseless and cowardly acts of violence. On June 19, 1972, Stuart Cohen, Sheldon Davis and Sheldon Seigel were indicted in the Southern District of New York for the bombing and charged with violations of 18 U.S.C. §§ 844(i) and 2. A superseding indictment, filed on July 3 and sealed until December 8, 1972, charged the original three defendants and a fourth, Jerome Zellerkraut, with the two counts noted above, and, in addition with conspiracy, and the unlawful possession of explosive devices, 26 U.S.C. §§ 5845(a)(8) and (f), 5861(d) and 5871.

§ 2. Principals

18 U.S.C. § 2

On February 2, 1973, three days before the expected commencement of the trial in the district court, the government moved to sever Sheldon Seigel from the trial on the grounds that Seigel was a government informer who had provided information leading to the indictments, that he had testified before the grand jury, and that he would be called as a witness at trial, under a grant of immunity. Seigel, through his counsel, moved for an order preventing the government from calling him as a witness on several, at once independent and connected, grounds — some novel, all complex. In essence, Seigel objected to any questions the government intended to ask him which were based on information gleaned from illegal electronic surveillance and violations of his constitutional rights. Pursuant to 18 U.S.C. § 3504(a)(1), the government affirmed the existence of illegal F.B.I. wiretapping involving Seigel. Accordingly, in response to Seigel's motion, the district judge commenced a taint hearing to determine the validity of Seigel's claims. On April 25, 1973, Judge Bauman denied the motion for a protective order and filed a careful, thorough and knowledgeable opinion in support of his decision.

§ 3504. Litigation concerning sources of evidence.

18 U.S.C. § 3504

(1) Upon a claim by a party aggrieved that evidence is inadmissible because it is the primary product of an unlawful act or because it was obtained by the exploitation of an unlawful act, the opponent of the claim shall affirm or deny the occurrence of the alleged unlawful act;

Defendants Cohen and Davis also made certain motions which the district judge considered during the course of the hearings. These motions are not under review at the present time.

Trial commenced on May 30 and, on the following day, Sheldon Seigel was called as the government's first witness. Apart from stating his name and address, Seigel refused to answer questions posed to him by the Assistant United States Attorney, and persisted in his refusal even after being ordered to answer by the court. Seigel was held in civil contempt, pursuant to 28 U.S.C.

§ 1826(a), and was released on bail. After the following witness, Richard Huss, was called, but before a question was put to him, Judge Bauman adjourned the trial for one week, during which time the government was directed to determine whether the Central Intelligence Agency had conducted electronic surveillance of several persons involved in the case and to so advise the court. On June 8, 1973, the government denied the existence of such electronic surveillance as to Seigel and all others involved in this case. It then agreed to vacate the outstanding order of civil contempt against Seigel, recalled him to the stand, conferred immunity upon him, and once again questioned him with respect to the Hurok bombing. Seigel refused to answer, in defiance of an order to do so by the trial judge, and was again

WANTED BY THE FBI

held in civil contempt. Release on bail followed once more. Richard Huss and Jeffrey Smilow were then called to testify as witnesses and, despite grants of use-immunity, they too refused to testify. They were held in civil contempt and committed to a federal detention center for a period not to exceed the duration of the court proceedings, but in no event in excess of eighteen months, or until they themselves decided to unlock the jailhouse door by agreeing to testify. 28 U.S.C. § 1826(a). Thus far, they have not chosen to do so.

These three judgments of civil contempt, dated June 8, 1973, form the basis of this expedited appeal. By statute, an appeal from an order of confinement for civil contempt must be disposed of as soon as practicable, and in no event later than thirty days from the filing of such appeal, 28 U.S.C. § 1826(b). The need for a speedy decision in this case is especially compelling because the trial, with the jury empaneled, currently stands in adjournment. The government has stated that its entire prosecution depends upon the testimony of these three reluctant witnesses — Seigel, Huss and Smilow — and that without their assistance, compelled or otherwise, the prosecution will be dismissed. The court, mindful of its ultimate responsibility, has expedited its decision by devoting its attention almost exclusively to this appeal.

I.

A few prefatory remarks on the posture of the case before us are appropriate. The legal issues involved in this appeal are set in a context that unfortunately highlights the seamiest aspects of the criminal law and its enforcement. Although the facts with respect to the criminal charge currently pending before Judge Bauman have as yet not been determined, the indictment concerns the commission of crimes which already have taken a grievous toll — the loss of a human life. The hearings conducted by the able district judge revealed the existence of two sets of F.B.I. wiretaps, which the government concedes lack any legal authorization. Judge Bauman also concluded that an automobile search involved in this case, conducted by New York City police, violated the Fourth Amendment. It was the court's judgment that the government's version of what had actually occurred in connection with the car search, "strain[ed] common sense" and was "patently unbelievable." The case also involves the use of an informer, always unpleasant business despite the conceded importance of informers for the administration of criminal justice. Given this context it should hardly be surprising to learn that the informer, Sheldon Seigel, adopted some of the tactics of those with whom he associated and himself surreptitiously recorded many conversations with a New York City detective to whom he reported, and on at least one occasion, even with an Assistant United States Attorney. Thus in the midst of so much deceit and lawlessness, we are called upon to render a decision that serves the cause of justice. When, under such circumstances, the court, as an engine in the pursuit of truth, is compelled to decide which of the two competing parties is more unbelievable, that engine is put under extraordinary strains in its effort to keep its commitment to the rule of law. In such instances, courts quite understandably would prefer to avoid any choice at all. Since this option is foreclosed to us, we proceed to a resolution of the issues presented.

II.

It is appropriate that Sheldon Seigel, the focus of so much investigative attention, and the principal subject of inquiry during the hearings conducted by the district judge, should occupy center-stage in this opinion. We shall discuss and decide his claims first and then proceed to a consideration of the Huss and Smilow appeals.

2 8 U.S.C. § 1826(a), the statutory provision under which Seigel was held in civil contempt, authorizes such contempt when a witness refuses, inter alia, to comply with an order of a court to testify, "without just cause." It is Seigel's assertion that he had ample just cause to withhold his testimony. Briefly stated, Seigel's view is that questions which the government proposed to ask him in connection with the Hurok

bombing derive from unlawful government electronic surveillance involving interception of his conversations at the Brooklyn offices of the Jewish Defense League and at his home. Furthermore, Seigel asserts that in connection with information discovered by means of illegal electronic surveillance, the government was enabled to elicit facts from him during his "informer" period, because of a massive invasion of his constitutional rights. In sum, his contention is that, in one way or another, he was coerced or pressured into cooperation with government officials, that such pressure stemmed directly from illegal wiretapping and ancillary constitutional violations, and that all prosecution questions asked at trial are tainted and, therefore, subject to suppression. With this summary in mind, we proceed to a discussion of the facts which are relevant to our decision.

On appeal, Seigel argues that the failure of the district judge to order the government to affirm or deny whether his voice was overheard by electronic surveillance conducted by various intelligence agencies under the control of the White House, the military or other agencies, when requested to do so on May 31, and June 8, 1973, was error. He also argues that he was justified in refusing to testify on the ground that the use-immunity afforded to him under 18 U.S.C. § 6002 and § 6003, was not coextensive with his privilege against self-incrimination, citing a recent case, In re Baldinger, 356 F.Supp. 153 (C.D.Cal. March 14, 1973), 13 Crim.L. Rep. 2029, and Harris v. New York, 401 U.S. 222, 91 S.Ct. 643, 28 L.Ed.2d 1 (1971); but see Kastigar v. United States, 406 U.S. 441, 92 S.Ct. 1653, 32 L.Ed.2d 212 (1972). In view of our disposition of Seigel's other claims, we need not reach these questions.

In October, 1970, acting solely under a direction of then Attorney General John Mitchell, the F.B.I. installed a so-called domestic security wiretap on the New York office of the Jewish Defense League. The surveillance, conducted without judicial sanction, continued until July 2, 1971. The government concedes that these taps were unlawful. It tells us that the tapes of this surveillance were destroyed, a fact not without significance, but that summary logs of the tap disclosed that Seigel had been overheard on six occasions.

On April 22, 1971, while the F.B.I.'s JDL tap was in operation, a bomb exploded at the offices of the Amtorg Trading Corporation, the home of the Russian Trade Mission in New York. A New York City Police Department investigation of this bombing, which we shall discuss at greater length in a subsequent portion of the opinion, led ultimately to physical surveillance of Sheldon Seigel, commencing on June 3, 1971, which in turn resulted in Seigel's arrest the following day, in a Manhattan parking garage. At that time, Seigel's car was searched — illegally as the trial judge concluded. The search disclosed fragments of wire, several pieces of plastic, a can of mace, a small film capsule filled with gunpowder, a cardboard tube with an attached fuse and ten empty alarm clock boxes. Seigel's automobile was impounded, and on June 29, 1971, he was indicted, on state charges, for possession of explosives.

The district judge's opinion relates the following subsequent events:

Seigel repeatedly tried to obtain the return of his car, without success. During these efforts he came in contact with a number of law enforcement officials, among whom were: Melvin Glass, then an Assistant District Attorney for New York County, now a judge of the New York City Criminal Court; Thomas Pattison, an Assistant United States Attorney for the Eastern District of New York; Michael LaPerch of the Alcohol and Firearm Division of the U.S. Treasury Department; and Detectives Santo Parola and Joseph Gibney of the New York City Police Department. All of these men, especially Parola, who was to develop a close and continuing relationship with Seigel, attempted to induce him to cooperate with various law enforcement authorities in their investigation of the activities of the Jewish Defense League, particularly with reference to the bombing of the offices of the Amtorg Trading Corporation on April 22, 1971.

These discussions between Seigel and government officials were conducted in the absence of his attorney, Harvey Michaelman, Esq., one
of the many attorneys who had volunteered their services to the JDL,
who had been retained by Seigel shortly after his arrest on June 4.
On approximately August 9, 1971, Detective Parola arranged for the
return of Seigel's car. Shortly thereafter, Seigel admitted that he had
participated in the Amtorg bombing and agreed to cooperate in the
official investigation of JDL activities. The circumstances leading to
this agreement merit some discussion.

During his direct testimony at the taint hearing, Detective Parola
stated that he had become familiar with the type of explosive device
used in the Amtorg bombing when one such bomb, which did not
explode, was dismantled by a member of the police department's
bomb unit. Analysis disclosed that wire seized from Seigel's car and
wire used in making the Amtorg bomb were similar. Parola testified — and we note that this testimony was given prior to a finding
by the district judge as to the illegality of the car search — that he,
and his partner Detective Gibney, met with Seigel some time during
the summer of 1971. In Parola's words: "We drove up and we did
speak to him in the car at that time and we explained to him that we
did find the wire in his car, and the gloves, and we did find — we did
trace component parts like the micronta timer that was bought in
the store in his neighborhood, and we related certain facts to thim
[sic] that we did have available that led us to believe that he was one
of the people who made that bomb." In describing Seigel's response,
Parola said: "At that time he just sort of looked at us in amazement,
and he said, 'How can I believe that this is true?' And we said, 'You
can take our word for it, we do have it, you know it was in the car,
you saw it was in the car.'" Parola related a subsequent conversation
which apparently occurred after the return of Seigel's car, in which
he said: "...we referred to the fact that we would like him to give us a
hand on the Amtorg case after telling him about the fact that we did

remove the wire, and we went into that phase of our investigation, that most of the wire and the gloves, and whatever we found in his car pointed to him as being one of the perpetrators."

On September 8, 1971, approximately one month after Seigel's agreement to cooperate with Parola, he was indicted by a federal grand jury in the Eastern District of New York for the Amtorg bombing. His "cover" was thus protected. Although Assistant United States Attorney Pattison, who was in charge of the prosecution, had stated in a note, given by him to Parola and then by him to Seigel, that Seigel would be given immunity in the Amtorg case, it is unclear whether Seigel knew that he could not be prosecuted under any circumstances, or believed only that he would not be prosecuted if he continued to cooperate with government officers. On one occasion Seigel indicated to Pattison that he wished to discuss his cooperation and the question of immunity with his attorney, Michaelman, but Pattison advised against it. Parola, by his own testimony, stated that he repeatedly advised Seigel not to discuss the question with Michaelman, or at least to get a lawyer who would be independent of the JDL. In any event, naming Seigel as a defendant in the Amtorg case prevented immediate disclosure of his informer status, a situation which served both the government's and Seigel's interests.

Thereafter, Seigel continued to speak frequently with Parola and Gibney, and to provide information concerning planned JDL activities against Soviet officials and offices. On December 15, 1971, however, without Seigel's knowledge, the government initiated warrantless less electronic surveillance on his home telephone, and the F.B.I. overheard many of his conversations. The surveillance, whose illegality is conceded by the government, was maintained through March 1, 1972. The dates, of course, are highly significant, at least in Seigel's eyes, inasmuch as the span embraces the date of the Hurok bombing, January 26, 1972. The tapes of these interceptions were also destroyed by the government. After the Hurok incident, Parola attempted to elicit information from Seigel regarding JDL involvement in the affair. It was not until May 7, 1972, however, that Seigel disclosed to Parola the names of the participants in the Hurok and Columbia bombings including his own. It is but another indication of the furtive and de-vious character of those who engage in these diabolical activities that Seigel himself had participated in the Hurok and Columbia bombings, even while serving as a vital government informer.

III.

At the threshold, we must consider whether Seigel should not have been permitted to raise the issues of illegal electronic surveillance and unlawful invasion of his constitutional rights, as a defense of "just cause" in refusing to answer questions during a criminal proceeding.

We need not tarry over the question whether Seigel has standing to object to questions on the basis of wiretap taint, despite his posture as a witness and not a defendant in a criminal prosecution. The gov-ernment concedes that such standing is conferred by statute, see 18 U.S.C. §§ 2510(11), 2515 and 2518(10), and inasmuch as the Supreme Court reached the same conclusion with respect to the more difficult question of a grand jury witness's standing, see Gelbard v. United States, 408 U.S. 41, 92 S.Ct. 2357, 33 L.Ed.2d 179 (1972), we believe the rule applies a fortiori to this case.

The district judge also concluded that Seigel had standing to object to questions based on violations of his constitutional rights, relying upon a recent decision of the Court of Appeals for the Sixth Circuit in United States v. Calandra, 465 F.2d 1218 (1972), cert. granted 410 U.S. 925, 93 S.Ct. 1357, 35 L.Ed.2d 585 (February 21, 1973), which extended the rationale of Gelbard to immunized grand jury witnesses who raise Fourth Amendment — other than wiretap — claims as a justification of their refusal to testify. Although in Gelbard the Supreme Court left open the question decided in Calandra, see 408 U.S. 41, 45, n.5, 92 S.Ct. 2357, 33 L.Ed.2d 179, the district judge concluded that "[to] rule otherwise would permit the government, when it has obtained evidence illegally, to confer immunity on a defendant and then circumvent the effect of the exclusionary rule by prosecuting him for contempt." The government contends that Calandra was wrongly decided. We need not decide the question, however, since the issue here is not so much one of standing to raise independent constitutional claims — as in Calandra — but rather the evidentiary relevance of the alleged constitutional violations to the issue of wiretap taint. We can hardly say that the district judge abused his discretion in expanding the scope of the hearing. The problem before Judge Bauman, as he viewed it. involved analysis of a chain of evidence. In his words:

The causal linkage [between illegal official activities] he [Seigel] perceives may be summarized as follows. The government first focused upon Seigel as a suspect in the Amtorg bombing because of conversations overheard on an unlawful wiretap installed at J.D. L. headquarters early in 1971. This knowledge, gleaned through wiretaps, enabled the government immediately to identify Seigel as the purchaser of a quantity of wire and batteries at a Brooklyn store called the Radio Shack on June 3, 1971. Thus Seigel was placed under surveillance on June 4, 1971 and ultimately arrested at the Meyers Brothers garage on that same day. At the garage Seigel's car was subjected to an illegal search, the fruits of which have already been described. This arrest, in turn, placed Seigel at the mercies of various government officials who further violated his constitutional rights by eliciting information from him in the absence of counsel, and who, indeed, actively discouraged Seigel from disclosing any of his meetings with these officials to his lawyer. In addition, the information was allegedly obtained from Seigel on the express understanding that he would never be required to testify, either in the Amtorg or Hurok cases. Thus Seigel argues that each link in the chain that led to his disclosures contains its own illegalities and is also tainted by the original illegality of the wiretap. I therefore propose to examine each "link" in turn.

Although Seigel contended that each "link" could, in itself constitute sufficient grounds to justify his refusal to testify, the links were also presented together as a continuous chain of wiretap taint. We conclude, therefore, that the district judge did not exceed his authority by considering the ancillary constitutional claims in the context of a wiretap taint hearing. Accordingly, we reach the merits.

Of course, the argument that permitting witnesses to raise constitutional claims will disrupt the orderly flow of court proceedings is inapplicable here since the trial would have been delayed in any event by the electronic surveillance taint hearing. The additional delay here involved was minimal. Arguably, Gelbard compels the district court to include consideration of alleged constitutional violations if they are ancillary to the wiretap claims. Otherwise, an aggrieved party might be foreclosed from effectively raising his claim of wiretap taint. We do not decide that question.

IV.

After reviewing the evidence, the district judge concluded that (a), Seigel's identity and participation in the Amtorg bombing were disclosed by an independent source and not by the illegal wiretap on JDL offices, and that Seigel's involvement in the Hurok bombing was disclosed by his statement to Parola and Gibney on May 7, 1972, and not by illegal wiretaps placed on Seigel's home telephone between December 15, 1971, and March 1, 1972; (b), the search of Seigel's automobile on June 4, 1971, which disclosed evidence linking Seigel to the Amtorg bombing was a violation of the Fourth Amendment; (c), no unqualified promise was made to Seigel that he would not be required to testify in the Hurok case since he received only a conditional assurance that the case would be "built around him" if possible; (d), no statements were deliberately elicited by surreptitious means from Seigel in the absence of counsel and, therefore, no violation of the right to counsel had been shown under Massiah v. United States, 377 U.S. 201, 84 S.Ct. 1199, 12 L.Ed.2d 246 (1964). Accordingly, the judge concluded that in the absence of any taint, Seigel lacked just cause to refuse to answer the government's questions at trial.

The government does not contest this ruling and we see nothing in Cady v. Dombrowski, 413 U.S. 433, 93 S.Ct. 2523, 37 L.Ed.2d 706, decided by the Supreme Court on June 22, 1973, to undermine it. We note here that the district judge prohibited the government from questioning Seigel on the basis of evidence seized unlawfully during the June 4, 1971, search. The court did not, however, indicate what line of questioning would be foreclosed by its ruling.

We conclude, however, that under the extraordinary circumstances that prevailed in this case, the government failed to sustain its burden of proving that information in its possession which formed the basis of its questioning of Seigel at the Hurok trial was untainted by unlawful electronic surveillance.

Our principal focus is the government wiretap on the offices of the Jewish Defense League in Brooklyn, maintained from October 1970 to July 2, 1971, a period that spans the Amtorg bombing, Seigel's arrest, on June 4, 1971, and the search of his car on the same day. In view of Detective Parola's testimony with respect to the use he made of the fruits of that search, and to which we have already referred in part III of this opinion, and Judge Bauman's conclusion that the search was unlawful, the source of Parola's knowledge of Seigel's identity becomes a question of substantial importance. In Gelbard v. United States, supra, in tracing the legislative history of Title III of the Omnibus Crime Control and Safe Streets Act of 1968 [hereinafter "the wiretap statute"] the Court noted that the protection of the statute extended even to the discovery of the identity of an individual through illegal electronic surveillance:

Congressional concern with the protection of the privacy of communications is evident...in the specification of what is to be protected. "The proposed legislation is intended to protect the privacy of the communication itself...." S.Rep. No. 1097, 90th Cong., 2d Sess., 90 (1968). As defined in Title III, "'contents,' when used with respect to any wire or oral communication, includes any information concerning the identity of the parties to such communicating or the existence, substance, purport or meaning of that communication." 18 U.S.C. § 2510(8). The definition thus "include[s] all aspects of the communication itself. No aspect, including the identity of the parties...is excluded. The privacy of the communication to be protected is intended to be comprehensive." S.Rep. No. 1097, supra, at 91.

408 U.S. at 41, n. 10, 92 S.Ct. at 2362 (emphasis added).

Moreover, years prior to enactment of the statute, this Circuit adopted the view that the government may not rely on the testimony of a witness that is based on the discovery of that witness's identity in the course of unlawful electronic surveillance, United States v. Tane, 329 F.2d 848 (2 Cir. 1964). Of course, the question is "'whether, granting establishment of the primary illegality, the evidence to which instead objection is made has been come at by exploitation of that illegality or instead by means sufficiently distinguishable to be purged of the primary taint.' Maguire, Evidence of Guilt, 221 (1959)." Wong Sun v. United States, 371 U.S. 471, 487-488, S.Ct. 83 S.Ct. 407, 417, 9 L.Ed.2d 441 (1963). Tane is consistent with that test, as noted in decisions of this Court in United States v. Cole, 463 F.2d 163, 171-172 (2 Cir. 1972), and United States v. Friedland, 441 F.2d 855, 860 (2 Cir.) cert. denied 404 U.S. 867, 92 S.Ct. 143, 30 L.Ed.2d 111 (1971). While these cases quite correctly assert that disclosure of an individual's identity in connection with one criminal act does not, by itself, preclude the government from ever using evidence of an unrelated crime in which he is involved, the rule survives that the government must show that evidence to which objection is made derives from an independent, untainted source and investigation. We can see no escape from the principle that a party raising objections to questions based on illegal electronic surveillance must be given a meaningful opportunity to argue that the evidence has been obtained by exploitation of the primary illegality.

This, of course, is nothing more than a restatement of principles so clearly enunciated in Alderman v. United States, 394 U.S. 165, 89 S.Ct. 961, 22 L.Ed.2d 176 (1969). Alderman established a procedure for conducting wiretap taint hearings. It asserted that:

When an illegal search has come to light, [the government] has the ultimate burden of persuasion to show that its evidence is untainted. But at the same time petitioners…must go forward with specific evidence demonstrating taint. "[T]he trial judge must give opportunity, however closely confined, to the accused to prove that a substantial portion of the case against him was a fruit of a poisonous tree. This leaves ample opportunity to the Government to convince the trial court that its proof has an independent origin. Nardone v. United States, 308 U.S. 338, 341, [60 S.Ct. 266, 84 L.Ed. 307] (1939)."

Alderman v. United States, supra, at 183, 89 S.Ct. at 972.

In the case before us, the government turned over summary logs of illegal electronic surveillance on the offices of the Jewish Defense League — maintained from October, 1970, to July 2, 1971 — and on the home telephone of Sheldon Seigel — maintained from December 15, 1971 to March 1, 1972 — and asserted that to the best of its knowledge, after full exploration, these were the only known wiretaps over which conversations of Sheldon Seigel had been overheard. The logs were prepared by FBI "monitors" whose function was to listen to the actual conversations, record them on tape and, from notes made during the conversation, prepare a summary. Six of Seigel's conversations were overhead on the JDL wiretap and numerous conversations of Seigel's were overheard on Seigel's home wiretap.

The actual tapes of these conversations could not be turned over to Seigel because, the government conceded, they had been destroyed. Nor were any transcripts of the actual conversations made. This concession is most troublesome for on another occasion a representation was made to a United States district judge that the policy of the FBI since 1968 has been to preserve electronic surveillance tapes, see United States v. Ivanov, 342 F.Supp. 928, 941 and n. 12 (D.N.J. 1972), on remand from the Supreme Court, 394 U.S. 939, 89 S.Ct. 1177 (1969). Indeed, Section 2518(8)(a), of the 1968 wiretap statute, the so-called warehousing provision, specifically provides that the contents of wire or oral communications intercepted under the authority of the statute shall, if possible, be recorded on tape and shall not be destroyed, except by order of the court, "and in any event shall be kept for ten years." The government could not ask for a clearer legislative intention and direction.

The significance of the destruction of this evidence cannot be understated in this case. To compel a party who objects to the use of evidence obtained as a result of unlawful wiretapping to go forward with a showing of taint, Alderman v. United States, supra, 394 U.S. at 183, 89 S.Ct. 961, and then to withhold from him the means or tools to meet that burden, is to create an absurdity in the law. The problem is particularly acute in this situation where no apparent reason for the destruction of tapes suggests itself, nor has one been suggested by the government. We recall in this connection that Congress specifically provided that under no circumstances may electronic surveillance tapes — even those obtained legally — be destroyed for a period of at least ten years. Individual rights, particularly the right of privacy so paramount in the minds of the drafters of the wiretap statute, cannot cavalierly be balanced away by other factors whether they be concern for efficient warehouse space management or different undisclosed reasons.

The government urges us to adopt the principle that considerations which bear on judicially authorized wiretaps are not applicable to the wiretaps presently under discussion, because so-called warrantless domestic security bugging not expressly held unlawful at the time these taps were installed, was not found to be invalid until the Supreme Court decided the question in United States v. United States District Court, 407 U.S. 297, 92 S.Ct. 2125, 32 L.Ed.2d 752 (1972). We are urged to hold, therefore, that the warehousing provision, 18 U.S.C. § 2518(8)(a), which requires preservation of records only for electronic surveillance authorized by Title III of the Omnibus Crime Control and Safe Streets Act of 1968, 18 U.S.C. §§ 2510-2520, does not apply to the wiretaps here under review. Since we do not today announce a per se rule that the government's failure to preserve the wiretap tapes must result in a reversal of these contempt orders, we need not decide the question. We note, however, that it would be a startling, if not preposterous, ruling that permits a more relaxed standard for illegal than for legal wiretaps. Such a precept would serve only to encourage illegal wiretapping. Moreover, since the warehousing provision of the statute, particularly in the light of Alderman, makes eminent good sense and serves the interests of fair play, in the context of this case the failure to produce the actual tapes, or accurate and complete transcripts of the overheard conversations so that Seigel could carry his burden at the taint hearing, compels us to strictly scrutinize the government's claim of independent source.

That claim with respect to the JDL wiretap was presented by the testimony of two government witnesses, Detective Santo Parola and Detective John McKeegan. The district judge clearly understood the significance of the taint question with respect to the first wiretap, since he permitted the government to reopen the hearings, over Seigel's objection, for the purpose of calling McKeegan to testify for the first time and, in addition, to have Parola return to the stand to clarify the nature of the police investigation which first brought Seigel to the attention of government officials. The government's version, accepted by the district judge, was that police agents had recovered an unexploded bomb from the Amtorg case and upon its dismantling, discovered that the bomb made use of a Micronta timing device.

Further, investigations revealed that timers were purchased by a man named Feldman at Radio Shack, Inc., in the Borough Park section of Brooklyn, one day prior to the Amtorg bombing. On June 3, 1971, Detective Parola of the New York City Arson and Explosion squad received a telephone call from the manager of the Radio Shack store who stated that Feldman had just purchased a substantial quantity of wire and a box of twenty-four batteries. The proprietor gave Parola the license number of the car, described as a gold Volvo, driven by the purchaser. A check of registration records indicated that the car belonged to one Irwin Seigel — a brother of the witness Sheldon Seigel.

Detective John McKeegan, who had been assigned to the Arson and Explosion squad in April, 1971, testified that he was present when Parola received the telephone call. He told Parola that the gold Volvo actually belonged to Sheldon Seigel. McKeegan, according to his testimony, had learned this information while assigned to the 19th Detective Squad during his own investigation of a fire bombing of the Iraqi Mission of the United Nations, which occurred on March 2, 1971. At that time, McKeegan interviewed a doorman in the building across the street from the mission who, when shown photographs at the Department's Bureau of Special Investigation, chose two as resembling the participants in the bombing, one photograph being that of Sheldon Seigel. McKeegan continued his investigation, visited Seigel's home in Brooklyn and noticed that Seigel drove a gold Volvo. For reasons unexplained in the record, no arrests were ever made in that case.

McKeegan further testified that he provided Parola with a photograph of Sheldon Seigel, which Parola showed to the proprietor of the Radio Shack store. He identified Seigel as the "Feldman" who had purchased the Micronta timers and the wire and batteries. Surveillance was commenced on Seigel which led to his arrest the following day.

Parola, who corroborated McKeegan's testimony, also noted that he never received information from wiretap sources concerning Seigel.

Thus, although the extraordinary good fortune of the New York City Police Department in this investigation must be considered nothing less than miraculous, the government's proof of independent source was, at least on its face, a strong one.

The government, however, was not the only party to engage in bugging in this case. Sheldon Seigel, by all accounts both devious and resourceful, tape recorded several conversations between himself and Detective Parola, one of which, occurring sometime in the fall of 1971, is particularly significant and revealing. The conversation, by its reference to the Amtorg investigation, reveals a different version of the manner in which the police learned of Sheldon Seigel's identity:

Seigel: Yeah, but on the first case if they wanted to drop it, they woulda dropped it already, they're just waiting around till after the second case is over, they just wanna, just wanna keep

Parola: They can't Shelly, it's horseshit, Shel.

Seigel: I know it's horseshit but

Parola: You know that

Seigel: I know, and they just want to keep me (inaudible)

Parola: All right. If we wanted to prosecute the first case, don't you think we got a good chance of knockin' you over if we really push.

Seigel: Not much.

Parola: Supposing I decide to testify, and I bring Joe [Gibney] up to testify. You know about the shit that was bought in the store and how we came to get all this information. You know it's done on wiretaps.

Seigel: What's that have to do with the first case.

Parola: 'Cause that's how we stumbled on to you. What do you think fingered ya? We did. We checked that store out again, and we found out you bought those batteries, and we said that you're up to no fuckin' good. We said we better watch this kid cause their up to no fuckin' good, and we never had your name before. Said this is a fuckin oddball name. We never had this kid before. That's how we stumbled on to ya. You know that. If you don't know that you're stupid or your fuckin' lawyer's dumb. Supposing me and Joey now turn around and say O.K. we told Mel Glass, listen, we're going to testify for you Mel, I'll tell you exact — [emphasis added]

Judge Bauman, referring to this passage in a footnote, discussed the government's claim that the critical phrase, emphasized above, should read: "You know it's not on wiretaps." In a rather puzzling explanation the district judge stated that there was "considerable uncertainty" as to what actually was said, that he listened to the tape several times and "reached the conclusion that the critical word was done," (instead of "not"), but that the context supports a reading of "not". This Court, however, which is in as good a position as the district judge to determine what the precise language was, listened to the tape many times over. We have concluded, without the slightest doubt, ambiguity or uncertainty, that Parola related to Seigel: "You know it's done on wiretaps."

Parola's words, therefore, must inevitably raise questions about the invincibility of the government's proof of independent source. If the New York City police department did learn of Seigel's involvement from a wiretap lead, the contents of those wiretaps, in the hands of Seigel's counsel at the taint hearing, may have dealt a shattering blow to the government's proof of independent source. For if wiretaps were indeed involved, Parola's in-court testimony on independent source, undermined on this critical point, would clearly have counted for little thereafter.

Of course, at this juncture we may only speculate whether the actual tapes would have revealed matters of importance which did not appear in the summary logs. But we cannot rely solely on the government's "good faith" representation on such a critically contested issue. Indeed, the government's good faith did not prevent illegal wiretapping here, nor did the government's good faith prevent it from searching illegally, or from narrating an account of the circumstances of that search which the court found to be incredible. In the face of Parola's own admission, speculation at this point only weighs against the government's plea that its claim be taken at face value. This "trust us to do the right thing" argument was roundly rejected by the Supreme Court in United States v. United District Court, supra. Moreover, we said in United States v. Smilow, that "[i]f government agencies are going to employ such surveillance techniques, responsibility for accurate description to the courts of the results of these efforts rests with those who make the report." 472 F.2d 1193, 1973. We are unable to conclude, therefore, that Seigel was not prejudiced by the destruction of the tapes. We believe, to the contrary, that destruction of that evidence effectively foreclosed him from fully pursuing the issue of taint.

The teaching of the Supreme Court in Alderman v. United States, supra, cannot be avoided. We are instructed that when illegal electronic surveillance has come to light it is the adversary system, not representations by the government and not in camera decisions by the court, which must be relied upon to determine whether overheard matter is "relevant" to the taint hearing. Here, the logs represent only a monitor's summary of the intercepted conversation. In a case such as this, however, with doubt cast upon the government's proof by their main witness's own admission of knowledge of the wiretap, we cannot ignore the significance to the adversary character of the taint hearing of the destroyed records. The Supreme Court articulated the reason eloquently:

"Adversary proceedings are a major aspect of our system of criminal justice. Their superiority as a means for attaining justice in a given case is nowhere more evident than in those cases, such as the ones at bar, where an issue must be decided on the basis of a large volume of factual materials, and after consideration of the many and subtle interrelationships which may exist among the facts reflected

WANTED BY THE FBI

by those records. As the need for adversary inquiry is increased by the complexity of the issues presented for adjudication, and by the consequent inadequacy of ex parte procedures as a means for their accurate resolution, the displacement of well-informed advocacy necessarily becomes less justifiable." Alderman v. United States, 394 U.S. 165, 183-184. 89 S.Ct. 961, 972 (1969)

While there is some evidence in the record indicating that the government agent in charge of the Seigel home wiretap, John Doggett, did not listen to the actual tapes but received only the logs from the F.B.I. "monitors," there is no evidence in that regard as to the wiretap of the JDL office telephone. The record is even silent as to the name of the government agent who supervised that wiretap. The government did not call any of the monitors to testify, although it represented at oral argument that the tapes were heard only by the monitors. We cannot accept these representations in lieu of evidence. Moreover, even had the monitors been called, or had the supervising agents testified, Seigel's ability to cross-examine would have been severely limited because of the unavailability of the actual tapes or, at least, a transcript of the intercepted conversations. Under the circumstances of this case, by which we mean Parola's own admission that he had knowledge of wiretapping, such limits would have been improper.

An apparently innocent phrase, a chance remark, a reference to what appears to be a neutral person or event, the identity of a caller or the individual on the end of a telephone, or even the manner of speaking or using words may have special significance to one who knows the more intimate facts of an accused's life. And yet that information may be wholly colorless and devoid of meaning to one less well acquainted with all relevant circumstances.

Alderman v. United States, supra, at 182, 89 S.Ct. at 971. We conclude, therefore, that under the sui generis circumstances of Seigel's case, destruction of the tapes or at least the failure to provide an accurate transcript of overheard conversations, denied to him the necessary armaments with which to pursue the adversary encounter contemplated by Alderman. Since the tapes are no longer in existence, remand for further proceedings would be futile. Accordingly, the order of civil contempt against Seigel is reversed and vacated.

V.

The appeals of Richard Huss and Jeffrey Smilow do not raise questions of comparable difficulty. Huss, who was called to testify on June 8, 1973, and granted immunity, refused to answer questions on the ground that Jewish law, which he observes, forbids him to testify against a fellow Jew in a non-Jewish court under the circumstances of this case. Judge Bauman rejected this claim on the basis of this Court's opinion in Smilow v. United States, 465 F.2d 802 (2 Cir. 1972), vacated and remanded on other grounds 409 U.S. 944, 93 S.Ct. 268, 34 L.Ed.2d 215 (1972), 472 F.2d 1193 (2 Cir. 1973). Although there are distinctions between the instant claims and those presented in the earlier case, they are distinctions without a difference to an American court. Accordingly, the order of civil contempt against Richard Huss is affirmed.

Jeffrey Smilow was held in civil contempt on June 8, 1973. He too argues that his refusal to answer questions was justified on the basis of Jewish law. That claim is rejected on the authority of United States v. Smilow, supra. Smilow also argues that by his testimony he is twice placed in jeopardy for the same crime. Since this appellant was not a defendant in the proceedings below, we utterly fail to comprehend his point. Moreover, he was granted immunity from prosecution based on his testimony thus eliminating any possible claim of self-incrimination. Kastigar v. United States, 406 U.S. 441, 92 S.Ct. 1653, 32 L.Ed.2d 212 (1972).

Finally, he argues that his refusal to testify was justified because illegal electronic surveillance of JDL offices disclosed conversations involving a person named "Jeff" and that destruction of the tapes compels a reversal of the order of contempt against him. The background facts are relevant here. In the first Smilow case, cited above, Smilow was held in contempt for refusing to answer questions before the grand jury investigating the Hurok and Columbia Artists bombings. The judgment was affirmed by this Court. In the Supreme Court, for the first time, the Solicitor General admitted the possibility of illegal surveillance when wiretap logs revealed conversations of an individual known only as "Jeff". The judgment was vacated and remanded, and this Court remanded to the district court for further proceedings. There the order of contempt was subsequently dismissed on the government's motion. In the instant case, when smilow was called to testify, the logs that might have some possible relationship to his conversations were turned over to him. They show six facially innocuous telephone calls, all on May 18, 1971. At that point, counsel requested the actual tapes and, upon being informed that they had been destroyed, stated: "Your honor, on this basis alone I would ask your honor to direct the Government to refrain from calling Mr. Smilow as a witness." On the ground asserted, the Court properly denied the motion. At no time did Smilow's counsel request a hearing, nor did he suggest that the government's questioning of Smilow had been tainted by illegal electronic surveillance. In fact, counsel's principal concern was the disclosure of tapes recorded by Seigel (not the government), of private conversations with Smilow, which counsel understood would form the basis of questions to be asked Smilow at trial. It was abundantly clear to counsel that Seigel, not the wiretap, was the source of the government's information concerning Smilow. Since Smilow never moved to suppress, nor even remotely suggested to the court that a proper claim of taint was before it, we conclude that Smilow lacked just cause in refusing to answer questions at trial. Accordingly, the order of civil contempt against him is affirmed.

VI.

In view of our disposition of the knotty problems presented to us, some final comments are required. It should be clear by now that the problem of electronic surveillance strikes deep emotional chords in a people whose concern for the protection of privacy — particularly the privacy of words and thoughts — is historic. In Title III of the Omnibus Crime Control and Safe Streets Act of 1968, Congress responded to this by balancing the needs of law enforcement against the important public and individual concern for privacy. It authorized electronic surveillance only under the most rigorous, carefully drawn standards. A cavalier, carefree and careless attitude towards the conduct of electronic surveillance makes a mockery of the labors of Congress to tailor the statute with precision. More importantly, it offends the spirit of liberty which has distinguished this nation from its birth.

The rule we announce today would not have been necessary had law enforcement officials simply preserved records of the surveillance tapes as the statute requires. The law imposes, in this respect, only the most minor inconvenience upon the government but which, at the same time, serves as an invaluable guarantee of individual rights. Adherence to that rule, even were it not mandated by law, would serve the government's interest for it would build confidence in its integrity and good faith. We often speak of governmental interests as opposed to individual rights. We should realize, however, that it is the government's principal duty to safeguard individual liberties if it is to continue to serve the people well.

Of course, we all suffer when, in Cardozo's classic phrase, the criminal goes free because the constable has blundered. People v. Defore, 242 N.Y. 13, 21, 150 N.E. 585 (1926). The remedy however is to help the constable not to blunder. The problem of crime, particularly the diabolical crimes charged in the indictment here, is of great concern to us. But if we reflect carefully, it becomes abundantly clear that we can never acquiesce in a principle that condones lawlessness by law enforcers in the name of a just end. There are those who argue that on occasion illegal methods must be employed to preserve the rule of law. Justice Brandeis responded eloquently to that argument and his words need no embellishment:

In a government of laws, existence of the government will be imperiled if it fails to observe the law scrupulously. Our government is the potent, the omnipresent teacher. For good or for ill, it teaches the whole people by its example. Crime is contagious. If the government becomes a lawbreaker, it breeds contempt for law; it invites every man to become a law unto himself; it invites anarchy. To declare that in the administration of criminal law the end justifies the means...would bring terrible retribution. Against that pernicious doctrine this court should resolutely set its face.

Olmstead v. United States, 277 U.S. 438, 471, 485, 48 S.Ct. 564, 575, 72 L.Ed. 944 (1928) (dissenting opinion).

We could not conclude without observing that the proceedings before Judge Bauman were conducted by him with superior craftsmanship and even-handedness. A capable trial judge, alert, responsible and intelligent government attorneys, and imaginative and able counsel for the appellant Seigel, explored complex factual and legal issues competitively, yet courteously, and always in the pursuit to truth. Recently, we have had occasion to comment in several cases on shoddy proceedings below. It is appropriate, therefore, to commend those who have exhibited an awareness of the virtues of adversary proceedings conducted in the respected tradition of our profession.

The orders of civil contempt against Smilow and Huss are affirmed. The order of civil contempt against Seigel is reversed and vacated.

ACKNOWLEDGMENTS

UNTIL ONE DECIDES TO WRITE a book, one does not realize the number of people who play a role in the final product. This is true even when one decides, like I have with both *Wanted by the FBI* and my previous book, *Because It's Israel: An Aliyah Odyssey*, to self-publish. Thus, I want to thank several people who read the original manuscript, critiqued it, made suggestions, and then reread the manuscript until I was satisfied with the final product.

Many thanks to my son-in-law, David Deutsch of New York, who critiqued the manuscript in far greater detail than I was anticipating he would do. While I certainly did not follow all of his suggestions (as they would have expanded the book to be much more than I ever intended), I think I have incorporated most of his recommendations.

Thanks to my daughter, Aliza Deutsch, an educator in New York and owner of Tiny Pumpkin Press, for her assistance in designing the book's cover.

I also want to thank my brother, Dr. Moshe Miller of Rechovot, Israel, and my cousin, Mark Schwartz of Phoenix, Arizona, who read the manuscript, suggested changes, and, more importantly, encouraged me to continue working on the book, believing that my story needed to be told.

While I have dedicated this book to my wife, Ronnie, for all that she has done for me over these past 53 years, I must also acknowledge her contribution of untold patience as I slaved away at the computer for so many hours, even when we had plans that I put on hold to complete a chapter or an important revision. More importantly, she was there for me when I risked arrest, permitting me to do what I thought was necessary to protect Jewish rights.

After the publication of *Because It's Israel: An Aliyah Odyssey*, many of my friends wanted to know how I did it. They had manuscripts, either complete or partially complete, and wanted to know how I got it on Amazon, as well as listed with booksellers across the globe. My response was simple. I sent the completed manuscript to Eliyahu Miller and his staff at JewishSelfPublishing, and he did the rest. Once again, he has come to my assistance in taking my manuscript and producing a beautiful book for sale around the world. Elisheva Ruffer was my editor, and her suggestions, corrections, and overall dedication to the project were invaluable to me. A special thanks to my publicist Stuart Schnee for his assistance in publicizing the book. I was determined to have Stuart on board lest I had any misfortune or accident, as occurred with *Because It's Israel*.

One of my former partners in New York, Sidney Kess, said I was the Jackie Robinson of the *shomer Shabbat* professional. If that is true, then I could not have done it without the support and assistance of my former partners in New York: Sidney Kess, Richard Stone, Paul Bodner, and Max Schein, all of whom I remember showing kindness and sensitivity to my religious observances. Finally, this story could not have been written without the incredible sacrifice of all those young members of the Jewish Defense League, inspired by their mentor Rabbi Meir Kahane, who gave me the opportunity to devote so much of my time and effort in support of Jews who needed help.

ABOUT THE AUTHOR

ARTHUR MILLER GREW UP IN New York's
Lower East Side, where he attended the
Rabbi Jacob Joseph School from first grade
through high school. He graduated from
City College of New York and Brooklyn
Law School, and he has a Master's in Law
from New York University.

While living in New York City, Arthur
became an inactive member of the newly formed Jewish Defense
League. As the JDL expanded its activities and became involved in
the Soviet Jewry movement, there was a desperate need for lawyers
to represent the numerous young JDL members who participated
in the group's militant activities. Miller was recruited by Attorney
Robert Persky to assist with these cases. At first, Miller refused, as
his practice was limited to tax law, but, ultimately, Miller was unable
to refuse Persky's desperate plea.

For the next few years, Miller donated hundreds of hours of representation to increasingly complex cases, doing battle with the FBI
and other federal agencies who were relentless in their attempts to
close down the JDL. Finally, in 1975, Miller himself became a target
of the FBI in what, to this day, Miller believes was the result of government-sanctioned antisemitism.

After keeping his story a secret for nearly fifty years, the treatment
of Jonathan Pollard forced Miller to go public.

Arthur lives in Bet Shemesh, Israel with his wife of more than

53 years, Ronnie. The Millers have four children, three of whom live in the United States and a daughter who lives in Bet Shemesh. The Millers' journey to Israel is the subject of Arthur's first book, *Because It's Israel: An Aliyah Odyssey.*

CPSIA information can be obtained
at www.ICGtesting.com
Printed in the USA
LVHW050756010621
689026LV00012B/1779

9 789657 041307